Twenty-four-year-old Jewel is truly a superstar. Her debut album, *Pieces of You,* has been one of *the* most talked about releases, selling over eight million copies. Her songs "Foolish Games" and "You Were Meant for Me" are loved by people of all ages all over the world.

Jewel's success reflects her determination to follow her dreams. From teaching herself to yodel at age six, to singing the National Anthem at the Super Bowl, to starring in a Hollywood movie, Jewel mesmerizes fans everywhere with her beautiful voice and captivating spirit.

But did you know . . .

- When Jewel was in the third grade, she got kicked out of class for yodeling.
- When she was fourteen, she was adopted by an Ottawa Indian family in Alaska.
- In high school, Jewel spelled her name Juel.
- She has dyslexia.
- Jewel is a hard worker—she has canned salmon, milked cows, chopped hay, modeled, and waitressed.
- While living in her van and playing coffeehouses in San Diego, Jewel had to wash up in Kmart bathrooms.
- She dated actor/director Sean Penn.

Find out *everything* about Jewel in this up-to-date tell-all biography:

Jewel: Pieces of a Dream

Look for Other Biographies from Archway Paperbacks

jewel
pieces of a dream

Kristen
Kemp

AN ARCHWAY PAPERBACK
Published by POCKET BOOKS
New York London Toronto Sydney Tokyo Singapore

AN ARCHWAY PAPERBACK *Original*

An Archway Paperback published by
POCKET BOOKS, a division of Simon & Schuster Inc.
1230 Avenue of the Americas, New York, NY 10020

Copyright © 1998 by Kristen Kemp

ISBN: 0-671-02455-8

First Archway Paperback printing October 1998

10 9 8 7 6 5 4 3 2 1

AN ARCHWAY PAPERBACK and colophon are registered trademarks of Simon & Schuster Inc.

Front cover photo © Sandra Johnson/Retna Ltd.

Printed in the U.S.A.

T 131197

To Jewel, and everyone else who has
encouraged me to follow my dreams

Special thanks to Julie Komorn, my editor; Steve Shaw, my husband; Chandra Czape, my friend; Ronnie and Carolyn Kemp, my parents; and to you, my readers.

Contents

Contents

Introduction

It's been a long journey for Jewel. From an Alaskan homestead to the cover of *Time* magazine, Jewel followed her dream.

The dream wasn't to be a rich and famous rock star. Actually, it was far more complex and far simpler. Jewel wanted to be happy. As a child, she wrote poetry and rode horses in Homer, Alaska, where she grew up without heat or electricity. As a teen, she studied music and art at one of the country's most prestigious schools. As an older teen, she ran off to San Diego to be with her mother. She thought her happiness would be there. It wasn't. After a string of dead-end jobs and depressing kidney infections, Jewel decided she'd had enough. She cut her bills to nothing by moving into an old VW van. She dropped out of society, knowing she could be gambling with her life. She sang in a coffeehouse to try to make enough money to eat and to keep gas in her traveling apartment. After a few months, she had fans.

Those fans crowded the little coffeehouse to hear the so-cool neofolkie from Alaska. She was hot—so hot that crowds stood out on the sidewalk just to see her. Record execs from Los Angeles had to push through the crowds to hear this nineteen-year-old sensation who was causing a stir in San Diego. They signed her to Atlantic Records and enabled this young woman to follow her dreams.

Jewel had figured it out. All she wanted to do was sing—that's what made her happy. Jewel was living her dream.

1

Life in Alaska

Yule Kilcher landed in the wondrous tundra of Homer, Alaska, escaping World War II's destruction in Europe. Legend has it that Old Yule, Jewel's grandfather from Switzerland, came down the Yukon River on a raft he made out of a raincoat. He arrived in America with plans to start an agrarian artists' haven for himself and his soon-to-be wife, Ruth, an intellectual Portuguese woman who also dreamed of pursuing a romantic, back-to-nature way of life. Yule borrowed money from his family and bought a large piece of Alaskan land so he and Ruth could start their own private culture-in-the-woods. It's the same spot of earth where a little girl named Jewel Kilcher would eventually grow up in her grandparents' tradition of sing-

1

ing, writing, philosophizing, and appreciating nature.

The Kilcher legend was only beginning. Ruth, who died in the summer of 1997 (the same week that Jewel was featured on the cover of *Time* magazine), wrote articles for the local newspaper and eventually got her book of poems called *Voice of an Initiate* published. As for Yule, he drafted the state charter, making Alaska the forty-ninth state to hang its star with the stripes on the United States flag. (It's no wonder that Jewel often refers to Yule as "one of the last pioneers.") And before he and Ruth divorced after thirty years of marriage, Yule also became a state senator, filmmaker, and lecturer. To this day, Jewel's family is considered an Alaskan entity. Her grandfather still lives on that Homer homestead and is a local celebrity; he's famous for riding to town on his horse-drawn buggy when his Subaru won't run. And he has nothing but kind words to say and fond memories to share regarding his superstar granddaughter.

Jewel's life story is the perfect continuation of the incredible Kilcher legacy. Here it is.

Shortly after May 23, 1974, the birth date of their daughter Jewel, life in Utah was over for Atz and Lenedra Kilcher. They decided to leave their college home in Payson, Utah, and head back up to the Great Northwest. The couple's destination was a tiny town called Homer, located on the Kachemak Bay in Alaska. Atz and Lenedra's hearts led them to that remote area, a place where Atz's family's past and future were meant to be.

This is the town where the first segment of Jewel Kilcher's made-for-TV-movie life took place. See, before superstardom, there was only a log cabin in the middle of an eight-hundred-acre Homer homestead. The young girl's existence was way more laidback *Little House on the Prairie* than fast-track *90210*. In fact, Jewel never expected or even dreamed of a glamorous life filled with fame and fortune. She was way too immersed in her parents' simple and earthy Alaskan ways to imagine that *she* would one day be the star of a sold-out concert tour.

Jewel's hometown of Homer is a close-knit community of 4,133 residents. It's one of the few places in the world where active volcanoes and mountainous glaciers can be seen simultaneously in one breathtaking, panoramic view. Fishing, especially for halibut, is the major pastime and export in the cold country. It's so frigid, in fact, that Jewel claims Easter as her favorite holiday "because it means that spring is coming." Once the warmer season arrives, the sixty-two-degree summer days are nineteen hours long. The weather is not without its benefits. The area is famous for the spectacular aurora borealis, nature's laserlike sky show that's known as the Northern Lights.

Jewel, like the other Homer townspeople, grew up with unbelievable environmental beauty and a Noah's ark variety of animals. She probably bumped into moose on Main Street, since that's where the animals tend to hang out. Other Homer natives include black bears, sand-hill cranes, and dozens of bird species.

Jewel passed her early days living a simple life off the land. It was during these years that she developed a wild passion for horseback riding—a skill she mastered at age two. Her favorite horse was named Clearwater. When she got him, he was sick and dying. "Everybody said he wouldn't live, but I just pampered and nurtured him," she says. She committed herself to making the animal well, and after many hours of loving care, Clearwater pulled through. Jewel had to bust her tail to keep him, working long hours to make sure he was fed and happy during the endless winters.

Growing up in Alaska was wonderful, but life wasn't easy for Atz and Lenedra's little gems— Atz Jr., their youngest; Jewel, the middle; and Shane, their oldest. In case you haven't heard the story (uh, like a million times), Jewel grew up on that Homer homestead with no heat, electricity, or running water. When other kids went home to play Pac Man on their Ataris or watch *He-Man,* Jewel went home to do chores, like canning salmon. The family ate what it could raise or take from the land. They raised cattle (they often ate cow-tongue sandwiches!) and had a garden filled with veggies. For a treat, they dined on Eskimo ice cream made out of blueberries and snow. Jewel told *Rolling Stone* that she was very proud of her natural way of life. It "shaped me into a certain kind of person," she said. Well, yeah, chores like hooking up a hose to a nearby stream to get water definitely upped Jewel's work ethic. Sometimes there would be worms in the water supply, but only if the stream had flooded the night before. Obviously, the hose method wasn't conducive to daily bathing. So Jewel and the other family members got to bathe just about once a week, especially in the freezing winter weather.

Because they had only a wood-burning stove, Jewel has said that "sometimes you'd wake up at five in the morning with frost on your eyelashes." That's how life was. Jewel would wake up, milk the cow, walk three miles down the road, and then hitchhike the rest of the way to school. She couldn't call anyone for a ride. Like many of their neighbors, the Kilchers didn't have a phone. Instead, there was a ride line on a public radio station. Everyone who used it had a handle, a nickname to use instead of a real one. So Jewel would listen to the radio and hear messages like "Two pigs in heaven looking for a king-size bed," or "To Miss Suzy Jane, you can't come by tonight." "If you're in the middle of nowhere, it's how you keep in touch," Jewel explained. Later, the family got a party line that they shared with all the neighbors in a ten-mile radius. Then when she picked up the phone, she'd hear everyone's conversations, and sometimes their secrets, too. Jewel admits that what she actually heard most over the party line was "Would you please get off the phone!"

Jewel has often referred to her childhood as poetic and romantic. "I was raised with a great respect for the land, how to work with it and understand it, and listen to the porcupine sound and hear the calling trees," she said in an interview for the book *Mindfire: Dialogues in the Other Future*. "And I was fortunate enough to be raised in a very nurturing environment," she added. A strong sense of family and community stemmed from their religion—the Kilchers were Mormons. Although they weren't strictly religious, there was a certain sort of togetherness that oozed from the family when Jewel was little. Some of her fondest memories are of marching with her father into the winter

wind on cold days. They'd go down to the edge
of the canyon and dig up willow roots. "They
were tangled and curly like a woman's hair,"
she said. The roots would be frozen, so she'd
have to take them home to thaw them out. Later
she and her dad would weave the roots into
baskets.

Jewel's father was a Vietnam veteran, social
worker, and singer-songwriter. Her mom was a
housewife, craftswoman, glass sculptor, and
former beauty pageant contestant. On the
homestead, the siblings shared a bedroom,
which inevitably made them close. Sometimes
Jewel found foreign writing in her journals and
poetry books, which meant her little brother,
Atz Jr., had gotten into them and composed his
own work. Yet another creative Kilcher.

Jewel has always thought in innovative, arty
ways. Her first memory is of herself in the
basement at her house, at the bottom of the
stairs, just before she was old enough to know
her name. Her mom was at the top of the steps
and said, "Jewel, how'd you get there?" In her
baby voice, she thought to herself, "Am I Jewel?" And all she could see was a flood of colors
swimming in her head. Then she said, "Yeah,
I'm Jewel." She understood her name, and a
little bit about herself. That vision of color has
inspired Jewel ever since. She sees herself as

myriad colors deeply embedded in her thoughts and soul—and songwriting.

Does that sound like poetry, or what? Many of Jewel's stories are just like that story of her first memory. Maybe it's because she's been studying poetry and philosophy since she was five. Every Monday night, Lenedra would round up the kids and conduct a poetry workshop. Jewel described the experience as "delicious." Not only did the family workshops fill her with warm, homey feelings, they also gave her much more—a ton of ideas. "It made my day fill up with more ideas and more thoughts and more observations. In that sense, it was like dessert," she said. She'd sit around and read the South American poet Pablo Neruda's poems, her all-time favorites. "I love them; they're fiery, passionate, full of revolution and love and lust . . . ah!" she said in *Mindfire*. Her love affair with poetry became evident to the world when she started writing song lyrics. Jewel calls poetry "the snakeskin of the soul." Like skin, her writing is constantly changing—and getting better, thicker, and more mature. Later, but not much (at this point, her age was still equivalent to her shoe size), she started studying the great minds of the philosophers Kant and Pascal.

Jewel definitely wasn't your average kid who got to watch gobs of TV. She might have been

2

Born to Sing

Jewel was very focused and determined at a very young age. If there was a challenge, she took it. If someone told her she wasn't allowed to do something, she proved them wrong. Her spunky, I'll-show-you attitude wasn't spiteful, and it wasn't an act. She merely wanted to overcome whatever stood in her way. It was almost as if she had been born with a sense of purpose. Her will to do whatever she wanted came automatically.

One of the first examples of this was when six-year-old Jewel playfully but seriously begged her father to teach her to yodel in the Swiss tradition. Atz told Jewel no, she needed to forget about yodeling for a few years. He thought she was too young—yodeling is incredibly hard on a child's undeveloped vocal cords.

11

Little Jewel did not want to hear that. She was going to yodel, even if it killed her. If her father wasn't going to teach her, she'd find someone else, or she'd teach herself. So she went to her granddad, Yule, to learn. Yule was the original yodeler in the family and showed Jewel the basics of his Swiss skill. Then she practiced her head off and learned to yodel in no time. "She was supposed to be sleeping, but she'd lay still in bed yodeling till midnight," said Jewel's aunt, Sharon McKemie. Her dad even remembers getting a call from Jewel's school when she was in the second grade. "They said she was yodeling all over and she wouldn't shut up," he said. Eventually, when Atz heard her mature, beautiful voice, he had no choice but to cave in. It didn't matter, anyway; she'd already taught herself to yodel. And, her aunt added, "Jewel's voice was stunning, even then."

When Jewel was six, the family took her on the road to perform. Atz and Nedra's pint-size singing sensation accompanied her parents to their local singing gigs. It wasn't a huge, unusual deal around their household. Jewel's parents were already seasoned singers on the local scene. They even had two records, 1977's *Early Morning Gold* and 1978's *Born and Raised on Alaska Land*. Bringing their daughter and their sons sometimes added to their folkie act. And

Jewel proved herself to be all about yodeling. Her dad says she had a real knack for the act. She learned fast, was tenacious, and worked hard. Atz told *Rolling Stone,* "One time when she was about six, she was yodeling with us at a hotel show, and this lady came up and said she was a professor of music. She told us it was supposed to be impossible for a child that young to be able to yodel—a child's vocal cords aren't developed yet." But Jewel's were working just fine, thank you very much.

Jewel remembers the touring schedule. "In the summers, we'd sing six days a week for three months straight, doing dinner shows; and then in the winters, we did concerts around the state." Jewel didn't tour with her parents all the time, but she was there for the majority of their gigs. They often performed at local hotels, like the Hilton and Captain Cook. They'd go on-stage, perform several songs, and then show a family documentary about Yule and the Kilcher heritage in Alaska. They also brought random instruments, like a homestead horn. "It was made out of a hose and a funnel that the brothers blew into—and made some noise!" said Homer resident and acquaintance Willy Nye.

Jewel loved everything about her parents' traveling show. "Those days were filled with butterscotch LifeSavers bought from hotel gift shops, waiting to go on, and talking with tourists from all over the world," she told *Interview* magazine in July 1997. Times were happy for the Kilcher family, and Jewel was thrilled about everything, especially about being a little star.

Right around that time, things weren't so sweet for Jewel at school. She was struggling with reading assignments and her other subjects, too. She got upset about it, especially the reading part. She loved to read, and when it became hard, Jewel didn't know how to cope. She was very young and was beginning to lose interest in life—it was becoming way too difficult for her. "I thought, what a bummer, my passion's all drained out of me," she said. So when she found out that all her problems were stemming from dyslexia, it was kind of a relief. Jewel added, "I was like, oh, that's what it was." Jewel was able to solve that problem—or at least to understand it and start working on it—and move on.

Her next battle was against a gymnastics coach. She actually got banned from a gym class because the coach said her coordination was awful. Jewel was peeved. She wouldn't accept that kind of comment being made about her. She knew she wasn't Shannon Miller, but getting kicked out of gym class? Whatever! So

Jewel went home and practiced her balance beam routine. She did it over and over, for hours at a time. When the routine was mastered, she headed right back to that coach. She showed off her vastly improved skills. Her coach was astonished.

3

A Change in Tempo

As Jewel found out, life is always unpredictable. The strong sense of family that existed among her brothers, her parents, and herself would never be the same after Jewel was eight. Her heart was broken—as was her home. Like millions of couples, Atz and Nedra got a divorce.

Jewel mainly lived with her dad, who stayed on the homestead. "It was very unreal. . . . Leaving your mom on a street corner while you drive away in the back of a car is just *brutal.*" Atz and Nedra had joint custody of the children, and Jewel saw her mother on weekends. Her mom moved to Anchorage, which is two hundred twenty-five miles from Homer. That's a four-hour car ride. For the Kilcher kids, especially Jewel, that meant an endless amount of time spent on the road in cars.

The whole ordeal was difficult. Jewel's life no longer seemed blissful, like the poetry she wrote. She wasn't able to see a psychologist—there wasn't money for that, nor was the subject even brought up. Instead, Jewel's writing became her therapist. So, Jewel and her journals became close friends. Now her passion for writing became a different story. Putting down her thoughts made her feel safe. No matter what happened in her life, even if she felt as if she'd lost a parent, she could never lose her ability to write. She became completely dependent on this talent. She'd write journal entries and poems, and "whatever," as she put it. She said she wrote very autobiographically, working only with the things she saw going on in her life. Her words linked her to the situations, so she could understand them. "It makes you familiar with your thought process, and your emotions and woes," she said. She grew addicted. "I think I became oddly dependent on writing. It started to become like a third limb or a sixth sense with me."

Even though Jewel didn't feel better right away, writing helped her ease the pain that comes with the devastation of divorce. She started dealing with her feelings and trying to understand them. But it wasn't easy. She was the only girl—in a house with three males. She missed her mother desperately. She missed life the way she'd known it. She missed Monday night poetry and singing together before every meal. Sometimes eight-year-old Jewel would make up little games with herself to cope. "I used to play a game where I'd pretend I was an eagle. I'd fly up and look down at my life and see how silly it all was, how everything would pass," she said.

The agony of divorce continued to linger, so singing became another form of therapy for Jewel. Jewel was no longer the cute little yodeling sidekick to her parents' act. This time, her singing was serious. At that point, Jewel's dad was the entertainer in the family, so Jewel tried to learn as much as possible from him. Not only was it a way to pass the unhappy hours, but it was also an attempt to get closer to Atz, and she admits to begging for his attention. She told *Rolling Stone*, "My dad, at that time, was out to lunch, bless his heart. And mean. So you're going to do anything you can to get on the good side of him."

Atz was struggling over the divorce, too. So he and Jewel bonded based on something they could both understand—singing. In his sorrow over losing Nedra (that's how Jewel refers to her mother), Atz drank too much. But rather than drowning in booze, he devoted some of his negative energy to the most positive thing he knew—his children, especially Jewel. He and his daughter decided to take their act on the road, just the two of them.

To prepare for singing in public, they started practicing five hours a day when Jewel was eight. "I sang my little brains out," she said. It didn't matter if her dad was yelling his head off or complaining about everything, Jewel kept right on singing with twice the determination she'd given the balance beam a few years earlier. Even when she was crying and upset by her father's words, she'd keep practicing. She loved singing and hoped that eventually it would help ease the tension. More important, though, she continued to work and respected her father. Jewel and Atz kept up the pace throughout the rest of Jewel's grade-school career, all the way to junior high.

"We'd practice—at my own will—for five hours a day," she told *Details* magazine. She always emphasizes that her father didn't push her into practicing and performing with him. She did it on her own. Jewel was the one into singing.

When it came to music, Atz was a perfectionist, both for himself and for his daughter. He believed that if people were paying to see them, then the father-daughter pair had to be the best they could be. "We rehearsed all the time striving for that perfection," she said. She respected her dad for that. Jewel remembers playing an AmVets show with him once when all the audience was handicapped and very drunk. It wasn't a cool atmosphere that day, and it didn't help that Jewel and her dad had gotten into an argument just before they arrived. Jewel got onstage and started pouting. "Nobody's listening anyway," she told her dad. He replied, "Jewel, you have to be professional. Don't bring your life up here. It doesn't matter. You're getting paid. You know, act professional."

Then a drunk came up next to Jewel and leaned over to whisper, "Stop looking so depressed." At that moment, Jewel realized a down-and-out veteran was telling *her* to cheer up. She realized she shouldn't take the good things in her life for granted, and she knew she would be all right.

When she was alone, Jewel would pore over her Ella Fitzgerald tapes, since the jazzy singer was one of Jewel's favorites. Then she'd sing over and over, recording herself until she got every single trill and loop of Ella's voice exactly right—until she sounded *exactly* like her. "That excited and thrilled me," Jewel explained. She also practiced singing with recordings of Kate Bush, Jennifer Warnes, Nina Simone, and Tracy Chapman. "They taught me complete control over my voice," she explained. It's no shocker that Jewel was able to perform sophisticated harmonies, like bluegrass, for example, at the tender age of eight.

Jewel compared "getting" her favorite singers' voices to mastering a color. "You can't paint with one color, you know, and so you take the yellow tone of Joni Mitchell's high warble and then take the purple of Ella Fitzgerald's stuff. . . . And then you use them all, you know. It just seems very visual for me. I see the lines and the colors in my head, and then my voice will draw it out. It's very much like painting for me," she explained to an interviewer on National Public Radio in 1995. Then she broke out into Ella to demonstrate her point—proving beyond a doubt that those five hours a day were worth it.

Alaska got to see the talents of the younger Kilcher while she traveled from bar to bar with her dad. As she got a few years older, patrons were starting to notice Jewel, but not always in positive ways. Sometimes nasty men would put coins in eleven-year-old Jewel's hand and tell her to call them when she was sixteen. These types of experiences shaped Jewel; she learned how to handle (ignore) these men. She also became a little rough around the edges, but at the same time sensitive to what other people (like those who are alcoholics) go through. Another negative experience that affected Jewel had to do with a man who'd seen one of Atz and Jewel's gigs. He approached Atz at a local store and asked to photograph Jewel. Her dad kind of knew the guy and was flattered, so he made her go even though she wasn't into it. When she got to the man's trailer, he asked her to put on a dress, and then he combed out her hair. Nothing bad happened, but Jewel went home and told her dad that she was very uncomfortable the whole time. Later, the same guy was in the paper as a child pornographer and molester. Atz came to Jewel crying—he told her he'd never doubt her instincts again.

All of the bars and swanky places where she and her dad ended up performing did have a positive effect on the youngster in the long run. She met people she knew she didn't want to become. She said, "I saw women who compromised themselves for compliments, for flattery; or men who would run away from themselves by drinking until they ultimately killed themselves." It was also good that her dad was there to help her understand why people said and did raunchy things. Jewel was learning about life.

* * *

One hotel owner, John Faulkner, hired the duo to perform at his Land's End Resort about twenty times over several years. She and her dad also performed for tourists at a few area hotels. Their act always included folksy, popular music, like the '60s song "Hang on, Sloopy." At the time, Jewel only knew about ten songs (now she knows hundreds). As for the rest of their act, Faulkner added, "Atz played the guitar; she'd just sing. They knew their act, had it down well, and people appreciated that. She just stole the show, though, especially when they yodeled."

4

True Teen

These years weren't easy in many ways, though. Jewel found solace in spending time outdoors. Riding her horses and working in her garden gave her tremendous "spirituality and comfort." When things were tough, Jewel realized that forming a bond with nature stirred something deep inside her. She explained, "No matter how hard my life with my family got, you knew there was some good force in the world, and you were a part of it." Despite her efforts to make herself feel better, she couldn't escape some of her problems.

Like puberty, for example. It just wasn't fun in a house with three guys. And to make matters worse, she had to share a room with her brothers. She couldn't tell anyone when she started her period or had other going-through-puberty pains. "I didn't tell anybody. You just kind of shave your legs in the dark by yourself, embarrassed," she said. Without a mother around to help her deal with these new issues, Jewel had a hard time keeping herself together.

This pattern of life had to be broken. A twelve-year-old girl—even headstrong, feisty Jewel—could only take a tiresome singing schedule and family problems for so long. Finally, Jewel had had enough and decided to hightail it to Hawaii, looking for an easier life than she had in Homer. "I was tired of the cold and my dad," she told *Rolling Stone*. She moved in with relatives and attended junior high at S. W. King Intermediate School.

Embracing her love for writing and the need to make a few friends, Jewel joined the school yearbook staff. She tried to fit in and have fun in the Aloha State, but it was impossible. For starters, she had bad personal experiences with racism—something she wasn't familiar with, considering her natural, accepting upbringing. Jewel was shocked and confused when she got beaten up for being white. "It was my first time dealing with prejudice," she said. So she wooed her classmates with her yodeling. At least they couldn't pick on her while they listened in awe to her unusual talent. She spent the rest of the school year in Hawaii, disappointed that things hadn't worked out a little better. Even though Jewel loved the warm weather, the local Hawaiian kids continued to be mean and unfriendly, making Jewel's life miserable. She couldn't take it; she was constantly being ridiculed for being different, the little white hippie girl from Alaska. "I was stuck there until I could earn enough money to go home," she said.

Finally, she got hold of some cash and went back to Alaska. Once again, she'd had it with life. This time, Jewel moved in with her mother in Anchorage. She was thirteen, and life changed dramatically once again. She didn't live on the homestead, and she had electricity, but she also had much stricter rules. Structure isn't always easy for a teenage girl who's never had any. Jewel says it was a hard adjustment to make, going from the freedom of her dad to the rules of her mother. "My dad was always like, 'Do whatever you want,' but my mom would say, 'Be home by nine.'" Of course, she wasn't thrilled, but she secretly respected the structure. Deep down, it's what she needed. She was with her mom; and she continued to do gigs with her dad on weekends. She was back home in Alaska.

It was just another afternoon to Jewel, an afternoon when she needed to get somewhere.

So she stood on a highway while visiting her dad in Homer and stuck out her thumb. She was hitchhiking. No, not everybody uses this method of transportation, but in Homer, it's not unusual to see kids doing it. Well, some kids—and Jewel was one of them. She caught the eye of a fellow Homer resident who just happened to be driving by. Lee Greene knew who the little Kilcher was, but he had never met her. He was immediately very concerned to see such a young girl with her thumb stuck out in the air. "I thought, 'Oh my God, this beautiful girl. Somebody's going to pick her up and . . . steal her. I mean, she was fifteen," he said. So he stopped his car, rolled down the window, and told Jewel, "What are you doing hitchhiking on the side of the road like that?" Well, Jewel had an answer for him. She reached down toward her feet and confidently pulled a knife out of her boot. To the stranger, Jewel said, "Would you [mess] with me?"

If this story doesn't describe her tumultuous teenage years, then nothing does. In fact, this little story defines Jewel's life. She can take on challenges, and she can take care of herself. As Lee said, "She always has."

As far as getting to school, Jewel often used her famous thumb (yep, she hitchhiked in Anchorage too). Or sometimes she just rode her mom's horses. In fact, she thinks everyone should use a four-legged vehicle. "We should ride something that's living instead of something that's emitting exhaust." When you don't have a car, as Jewel didn't, that's exactly what you do. Jewel even rode her horse to her part-time high school jobs.

Jewel had other adventures that kept her busy during her early teen years. Perhaps the most influential one was when she got adopted by Ottawa Indians. When she was fourteen, she started hanging around with a group of Native American Alaskans and was greatly inspired by their spiritual teachings. "My mother was always spiritually guided and has always had the strength to listen to herself and her heart. I was raised with a sense of magic, and also a very deep appreciation and love for the Indian way," she said. So, when her heart started to crave that same sort of spirituality, she went for it. She started to make friends with the Native Americans and participated in dances and drum circles.

Here's how the adoption works. You attend a gathering, and *you* adopt the Indian way. She has often said it really wasn't a big deal. You go to a powwow, and then everyone in the group becomes your aunts or uncles. Two huge Ottawas guided Jewel and became her mentors. She half-jokes that the wives of the two Ottawas were worried that their husbands liked Jewel, so there may have been some animosity that eventually led Jewel to stop hanging around. Before all that, she was into the whole thing and learned important lessons from the tribe.

One day, the uncles took Jewel up on a mountain and told her the story of the White Buffalo Woman, who carried the peace pipe to the first American Indians. She was beautiful, with long hair, and as she danced across the meadow to two young braves, she told them, "I have something to give, who will take it?" One aggressively went for the woman—he wanted *her.* The other stayed back, waiting patiently. Immediately, the Buffalo Woman knew she wanted the man who had humility—the one who waited. The moral behind the story is that she had the wisdom to know the difference between them. The uncles told Jewel she needed to learn from this story, that she needed to speak more from her heart and listen to what it told her to do. Further, they had a premonition that she has remembered ever since. They said, "Jewel, you have a gift to give to the world, but first you have to learn."

As far as learning, Jewel did plenty of that

while living with her mom in Anchorage. If not the Indian way, the hard way. Like most girls in high school, she went through many stages. All within about two years. She was, believe it or not, a prep for a while. Another phase was totally '80s—she dressed in silk shirts, wore blue eyeshadow, and even permed her hair. Rumor has it that she also listened to Cyndi Lauper. But that phase didn't last long. Jewel wasn't suited for a Molly-Ringwald-*Sixteen-Candles* life, and she knew it—she didn't want one, anyway. Another phase was a bit wackier but was getting closer to the real Jewel. She wore '40s-style pillbox hats and vintage clothes. In the ninth grade, she joined a rap band called Le Creme, where she was known as Swiss Miss. Her boyfriend Damien was in the band, too. They were all into hip hop, and to this day, Jewel can recite "Big Daddy Kane." And she sings a mean version of "Pimpin' Ain't Easy."

Jewel dated all kinds of guys in high school. Her boyfriend Damien was black. When her father first met Damien, he cried. "He said he was so proud that he had raised such an open-minded daughter," Jewel said. She embraced the differences among races and went out with a Thai boy, a Sri Lankan, and tons of other boys, too. "I'm not as much a strong feminist as I'm a strong humanist," she said. She wasn't afraid to be open-minded, nor was she afraid of the things less open-minded people would say. Besides, why did she care what other people thought about her boyfriends? One day, she'd date Sean Penn.

Despite the phases and the boys, both of which came and went super fast, one thing was a constant during Jewel's high school career: She stayed very involved in philosophy. She had always studied and had a passion for it. So did Nedra. In high school, Jewel really threw herself into it. She said, "What philosophy can do for people is amazing. It opens your mind."

Studying philosophy was challenging for her because of her dyslexia. But, as usual, that just made her plug away harder. She learned to pick ideas apart to learn them more easily. "As a result, I'm very aware of how I get through things," she says. Jewel thought her method of learning would make her a great philosophy teacher. And she was right. Soon she was helping her own teachers conduct seminars about her favorite philosophers, like Pascal and Kant. She even ended up teaching the teachers and also taught *The Velveteen Rabbit* to second-graders. Philosophy enabled her to do these things. "But eventually it became a trap for me—I started to give reason too much credit," she says. Philosophy sometimes focuses on consistencies in life. And sometimes, no matter what you do, life just isn't consistent, especially not for Jewel.

Just as she was getting settled with her mother in Anchorage, life took yet another brutal turn—Jewel reported in an interview that her mom was questioned by the authorities. The whole incident is unclear but it purportedly had something to do with shady dealings by one of Nedra's business associates. (Jewel's mom was a glass artist.) Jewel said the investigation was just awful. In a *Rolling Stone* interview, she said, "Investigators would come to my school, and there would be things on her in the paper. We eventually ended up having to hock our stuff and move two hundred miles away." Jewel's mom adamantly denies this ever happened, claiming Jewel was misquoted, and very little information is available. For whatever reason, when Jewel was sixteen, she moved again. This time, she ended up in a tiny town called Seward.

Jewel was becoming antsy again. It was time to find a place where she could be herself. In Seward, she started feeling as if there had to be a purpose for her life, but she hadn't found it yet. "I kept thinking, what am I going to do with myself?"

While trying to figure it out, she learned of a

friend who was attending Interlochen Arts Academy in Michigan. After conducting a little research, she knew that she wanted to go there, too. There was one huge problem, though. The Kilchers were known for their rich history, not their riches. Neither parent had enough money to send Jewel to that school, no matter how talented she was. So it really didn't look as if Jewel had a chance of going to the famous, elite, artistic high school. In true Jewel style, she pushed forward; as always, she was determined. Jewel would get her way.

After a lot of thinking and concocting, Jewel thought of a way she could get to Interlochen. It wasn't too hard, really. She decided to put on a show and raise the cash herself. Her mom and aunt jumped in to help her. They set their sights on Homer, where Jewel's roots were and where she often visited and performed. They cooked up a big show at Atz and Lenedra's old hangout, the Land's End. The whole town pitched in and contributed. Jewel's benefit show was a success. She raised quite a stash, and the rest of the money came from Interlochen. Not only was she accepted into the exclusive school, but she was also given a six-thousand-dollar vocal scholarship. She decided she would earn whatever other money she needed with part-time jobs in Michigan. Only one thing really mattered now: she was going. At that time, she didn't realize that she'd never live in Alaska again. Just like that, Jewel set out for, possibly, her most life-changing journey of all.

5

Interlude at Interlochen

Going to school in Michigan was not easy, but at least Jewel had been far from home before and didn't freak as much as her homesick classmates. Interlochen is basically a boarding school, where most of the students live in dorms. So not only are kids away from their families, they're also attending a high-pressure, world-famous arts academy that boasts graduates such as actresses Linda Hunt and Meredith Baxter Birney. It was a difficult, challenging school, which was cool with Jewel. It was hard to get into and even harder to stay in. The students had huge work loads—kind of like college. One teacher said it's nothing for kids to finish dinner and then do homework until two in the morning. It takes a special student to handle all of this with finesse.

Jewel was one of those special students. She was happy just to *be* at Interlochen. She definitely wasn't like the majority of students whose wealthy parents had no trouble with the sky-high tuition. Jewel worked hard for everything in her life and had done the same just to get her Alaskan butt to Michigan. Challenges were welcome to her, even fun, because Jewel was always ready to try new things. Studying at this prestigious school presented Jewel with a tremendous variety of exciting adventures. (She could handle them all, no problem.) Even if she had to spend more time reading and studying than most kids because of her dyslexia, at least singing didn't give her trouble. In fact, the arts in general were easy for Jewel. For the second time in her life, she became a star. Only this time she did it all by herself. She wasn't hanging on the apron strings of Mom or Dad.

Jewel arrived at Interlochen in the fall of 1990 and attended Interlochen for her junior and senior years of high school. It *was* unusual for a student to take the school by storm, and that's just what Jewel did. She got accepted knowing she was going to study vocals, but she thought the focus would be on blues. One small problem—they didn't exactly teach pop music at this art school. So she ended up studying . . . opera. When she arrived, the first thing Jewel had to do was sing an aria. But she didn't even know one. Jewel went to her voice teacher and asked how to go about performing one. The teacher asked Jewel which language she'd like to sing in. Jewel answered, "French." Next thing she knew, she was in a school recording studio, in disbelief. She thought, "A nice little French aria—this is a joke!" To her surprise, she was accepted into the French opera program, all before she really knew what was going on. She did exceptionally well at opera but found it slightly scary. "I'm not putting voice lessons down at all, but it started changing my voice in a way that became unspontaneous—very correct but very emotionless," she explained. Jewel pleaded with her voice teacher, Nicole Philibosian, to be allowed to skip some of her lessons. Philibosian, who adored the young woman, said, "We're pretty open, but we don't teach blues and pop singing. But here she was, so what were we going to do with her? We taught her what we could, and we're very glad she was here." Taking it easy on opera lessons, even though she excelled at them, allowed Jewel to pursue her other Interlochen interests, such as drawing, sculpting, dancing, acting, and anything else she could throw her creative self into. To keep her scholarship, Jewel had to show up to do opera performances—which was the fun part, according to Jewel.

Philibosian thought Jewel was so talented that she wanted to take her to France to study opera with the world's finest artists. Jewel's voice eventually would be good enough to compete against the best French opera singers in the world, according to her teacher. "I almost did it," Jewel admitted. "But you have to wait until you're thirty, generally, to make it. You have to wait for your voice to mature." Jewel wait? No way. "I thought that I'd rather have a place where I could speak a little bit more and speak in my own notes and my own words," she explained. This is when Jewel started writing her own music. She even started performing gigs on her own at local coffeehouses.

Here are some of the comments Philibosian made on Jewel's permanent Interlochen records during the two years she taught her.

January 14, 1992: "Sometimes the master gets taught by the student! Jewel is, as usual, a bright spot in our studio. [She] is incredibly excited about learning and how to make beautiful sounds."

March 14, 1992: "I am very proud of Jewel for tackling a very difficult assignment and going ahead with her recital jury. She can be proud of her accomplishments and the progress she has made, which is remarkable. There is far to go, vocally, musically, and in presentation, but her unique talent is really showing itself to all of us. BRAVA!!"

Usually, students at Interlochen are pretty much bound to one major—especially because the school is so stressful and kids have to focus in order to succeed. Obviously, Jewel didn't follow those rules. She wanted to get into acting class, and voice majors weren't allowed to do that. Robin Ellis, the drama teacher, says Jewel came up to her one day and "expressed eager interest in taking my class." That semester, Ellis actually had a few extra spots in the beginning course, and she decided to give such an enthusiastic student a chance. Jewel was allowed to audition for Ellis and the principal. Her performance was convincing and got her into the class she was dying to take. "She was the first student we tried this with, we decided we'd see how it went," Ellis added.

To the surprise of everyone (well, except Jewel), she quickly took the role of class leader and easily outshone the acting majors. "Jewel had so much energy and was so curious and eager," Ellis said. She was impressed by Jewel, a sixteen-year-old with so much initiative. "Jewel created opportunities for herself, she made things happen. If she hadn't come to me and asked to be in acting, she never would've had that experience. And once she was in my class, she wasn't content to just be there. She had to be the best. Jewel didn't get B's," Ellis explained. Her abilities landed her the lead in the class play, *The Spoon River Anthologies,* based on Edgar Lee Masters's collection of monologues about a bunch of ghosts from a town called Spoon River. They sit on their graves and tell their life stories. Jewel played the most prominent ghost, an elderly woman. And according to her teacher, she did on excellent job. "She was much better than the average student." She also unknowingly got the other kids a little jealous, too. After all, who was this voice student who barged into the acting class and took control? But Jewel was unaffected by their resentment. Her attitude was way too positive to be brought down by petty jealousy. She wasn't braggy about her ability to act, but she didn't apologize for her talents, either. Jewel was proud to be the best. Besides, Jewel could care less what other people thought. She was a bit of a loner and a "free spirit." Every year after that, Ellis let in two students who weren't acting majors. Eventually, there would be an entire class for nonmajors. "Her success in the acting class paved the way for nontheater majors. I love teaching it, too; it gives me a chance to get to know students who aren't in my division," Ellis added.

Here are some of the comments Ellis made on Jewel's school record.

November 1990: "Jewel is a tremendously

valuable member of our class, and an exemplary student. Her quiz and paper scores set the standard for the class. She is committed, eager, highly motivated, and seizes whatever opportunity she can. She participates in class without hesitation and shows a lot of promise as an actor."

January 1991: "Jewel consistently produces quality work. She shows a sincere dedication to learning. I look forward to her continued growth."

All of the teachers who became acquainted with Jewel fell in love with her. Including the sculpting teacher, Jean Parsons. It was a fluke that they even met. Jewel needed extra money to help pay for her tuition, and a friend of hers, a sculpting major, talked her into modeling for a class. All she had to do was sit still for hours at a time—as if study-pressed Interlochen students had tons of extra time—and wait for students to sculpt, paint, and draw her likeness (fully clothed). It wasn't exactly the most sought-after job. Parsons says that she had trouble finding willing students to do it. But Jewel needed cash, so pose for hours she did. "Jewel even came in on Sundays so the kids in the class could get extra work done," Parsons said.

She started becoming really good friends with kids in the class. Parsons said Jewel won everyone over with her stories of her home in Alaska. "She used to say how cold it was, and how many miles she'd have to walk to get to a bus that took her to school. And, of course, she yodeled all the time." As the semester went on, the conversations between Jewel and her classmates became more in-depth. That particular class was very close. Jewel even shared the following information one day while posing: in order to pay her school bills, she had to sell one of her favorite horses.

Parsons and Jewel became buddies, too. "Well, when you first meet Jewel, you just don't know how to take her. But I got along swell with her. She was very level-headed, and she had an independent spirit. She was sincere and thought-provoking," Parsons said. Shortly after Jewel told the class about losing her horse, Parsons received a mail-order offer for a free art instruction video—it was all about famous horse paintings. "And so I thought of Jewel," Parsons explained. She ordered the video and had the entire class over to her house one Saturday afternoon to learn about famous horse paintings.

The class had a wonderful and comfortable rapport. Parsons said she even encouraged Jewel to pursue her own interests during her modeling time. "It's pretty boring and time-consuming, so I told Jewel she could bring her guitar if she wanted to," the sculpting teacher added. She couldn't play very well, but she started writing little tunes for herself that semester. Eventually, some of those tunes wound up on an album called *Pieces of You*.

The next semester, she didn't have to pose anymore, and Parsons didn't see much of her—until she actually joined the sculpting class. "She had picked up a lot of information while modeling, and she became interested. Next thing I knew, she was in the class," Parsons explained. The two were such a pair that Jewel even thanked her on her first CD. Parsons didn't know about it until a recent class told her. She was so moved that she bought the CD (she didn't even own a CD player) and marched over to Interlochen's student-run radio station. She demanded that they put on the CD, even though the station is all classical. "That was my gift to her; I wanted to make sure they played it."

Another story of Jewel's winning over her classmates originated in her dance class, where, once again, she was one of the better dancers. Dee Smith, a faculty member, would pop into the different classes to see what everyone was up to. "One time, I was in the dance building, I remember stopping when I saw Jewel go over and stand next to the piano after her class. She just stood there and yodeled, and her classmates all stood around and listened. They clapped at the end. That's not something you see that often, I won't forget it," Smith said. Jewel's level of talent was amazing. Even back then, Jewel knew exactly who she was. She was the girl from Alaska who was one of the only double majors (voice and sculpting) and one of the only students who excelled at everything she tried. Jewel could do no wrong.

Well, most of the time. She was known for being a little mischievous when it came to the dress code. She'd show up at choir practice wearing gladiator sandals with straps that wrapped all the way up to her knees. She never caused trouble or anything, but Jewel, like lots of the other students, did have to be reminded of Interlochen's dress code. She'd push it as far as she could. Also, Parsons and Ellis both remember Jewel walking around campus barefoot. "She liked to do things a little differently," Smith said. She even changed the spelling of her name from "Jewel" to "Juel" during a phase in high school (she went back to the original spelling when she left high school). Jewel had friends, but she wasn't into cliques and crowds. She was too focused on her future goals—like writing music—to be consumed with the social scene. Jewel didn't care about the strict rules of high school etiquette or about wearing "cool" clothes and makeup. She never painted her nails or acted prissy—she was extremely natural. That stuff wasn't what she was all about, then or today. Ellis said, "She was a free spirit who was a little bit on the rebellious side. She was a unique little flower and also a strong individual. She seemed very sure of herself at a very young age. She was going to dress the way she wanted and be the way she is, and not apologize for it." Jewel was too busy keeping busy even to notice or care that she didn't quite fit in.

For one, she was teaching herself to play guitar. She knew she needed to learn, now that her father wasn't there to strum the tunes for her. Jewel wanted to keep doing gigs on her own, but at the time, she didn't dream she'd be playing guitar for the masses. "I only started so I could hitchhike across Mexico doing Bob Dylan songs," she admitted. Learning guitar was difficult for her. Again, dyslexia reared its ugly head. She said the learning disorder only made her practice twenty times harder. The basics did come quickly because she spent a lot of time practicing. Before she knew it, she was doing shows in nearby Traverse City and at the Interlochen student coffee shop. She often yodeled and carefully strummed the very few guitar riffs that she had learned. Philibosian remembers one particular time when she was struck by Jewel. "Jewel was just getting ready to leave Interlochen, and she said, 'I'm going to sing in Traverse City tonight, do you wanna come hear me?'" When Philibosian got there, Jewel looked at home at the coffeehouse while playing a guitar. "Jewel just blew me away. I just sat there with tears running down my cheeks. Frankly, I learned a lot from Jewel."

Jewel's biggest high school gig by far was in 1992 at New York City's Lincoln Center. Of course, her most famous appearance at the arts complex was a few years later in 1996 when she played Dorothy in a rock-opera version of *The Wizard of Oz*. Most people didn't realize that Jewel had been there before and was already familiar with the center. She was a member of the Interlochen choir—which was exceptionally talented. So talented, in fact, that Lincoln Center invited the choir to participate in its Mozart bicentennial celebration. So there was Jewel singing from the back row, lefthand corner. Little did she know that in a few short years, she'd be the star in the center of that very stage, singing "Somewhere Over the Rainbow" in Judy Garland–like glory.

Eventually, it was time to leave Interlochen. Jewel had to move on. Here's the final comment her voice teacher made on her record.

May 27, 1992: "Brava, little diva! You're off to a big future, and we're glad that we've been able to contribute to the quality of your voice by having you here. Please remember that your voice needs to be warmed up so that it can have the stamina that your career will demand, and don't forget your *hums* and *vuvs*. We'll miss you. Good luck!" This teacher, the one who'd seen her perform at the coffeehouse, knew what Jewel's future would hold. She knew exactly what her Alaskan opera student was capable of doing.

Jewel was extremely grateful for the encouragement, teaching, and friendship she received at the school. She thanked her teachers, something most students don't take the time to do. Parsons said Jewel sent her a "lovely letter" right after graduation. Jewel kept in touch and wrote her sculpting teacher from California. She also gave a handwritten note to Ellis, thanking her for the acting class and for how much she learned from it. On the card, Jewel drew a picture of her horse, with a picture of herself standing in front of it. She also wrote a little story to Ellis that made an analogy between breaking a horse and teaching Jewel to act. It had been hard for Jewel to take direction and learn acting techniques. "Jewel was just thanking me for what she learned," Ellis remembered. "You've got to have an impact on students to be a worthwhile teacher. We really treasure those students who do take their time to express their appreciation. So Jewel's note is very personal, and it means a lot to me."

Jewel sweetly signed the note to Ellis, "I love you, Juel Kilcher," and on the back of the card, she drew a cute copyright symbol that said, "A division of Juelmark." Ellis joked, "It was like she had this premonition that she'd be famous one day."

6

To San Diego

So, high school was over. Now what? Jewel wished she knew the answer. After Interlochen, she felt a little lost. She didn't know if she should go to college, get a job, or follow her seemingly unrealistic dream to sing professionally. After some serious thought, she ruled college out. In the book *Mindfire,* she talked about it: "I didn't know what I was going into. I would have appreciated a mentorship." She liked the idea of an old-fashioned apprenticeship, where she could learn a trade from an accomplished adult. Since those are rare, Jewel had to make a decision. She was restless and felt like "a bird needing to fly south," she said. "I just didn't know which direction was south."

As far as college was concerned, she says, "I knew I didn't want to go. School was hard for me." Besides, there was no spark in Jewel for college. The whole process—applying, spending tons of cash, and studying subjects that wouldn't be useful to her—was repulsive. "I felt resentful that artists have to go to school to be artists," she told *Interview* magazine in July 1997. She finally decided to go where her heart was—which was with her mother, who just happened to be in San Diego at the time. "I wanted a sense of purpose in my life, and I thought maybe I would find it with my mother," she says.

She started her journey to California exactly as she'd begun her journey to Interlochen— poor. She had to sing on street corners for money to even get to San Diego. Eventually, she had enough to take the train. Upon arrival, she still didn't find any answers to the question of what she was going to do with her life.

The first thing on her agenda was to make some money. She wound up with a series of low-paying jobs to help her mother pay the bills in their tiny one-bedroom San Diego apartment. She hated them all—she waitressed, worked as a salesgirl and also a receptionist. These jobs weren't challenging, fulfilling, or getting her any closer to happiness. Sometimes, her bosses would ask her out to dinner, and she was so poor and hungry that she'd go out on

says. The Mexican police told the couple to come along with them. Once out on the water, Steve and Jewel got to talking with the armed officials and asked them what they were working on. Their answer: they were in pursuit of drug dealers.

Jewel asked them if they were about to be involved in something dangerous. The cops answered something like, "Yes, there's usually a lot of shooting when we make these arrests." It wasn't too much later that the *federales* found suspicious-looking subjects in a boat along the shore. They started speeding toward it. They handed Jewel and Steve automatic rifles. Jewel said, "And here I am, in a bikini, saying, 'Are you sure this is proper procedure?'"

When they got ashore, the couple ran to safety just as the shooting started. Eventually, the police snagged their smugglers, but they didn't find even one ounce of drugs. Everyone could smell pot, though. Jewel and Steve were stuck on this foreign shore with no clue how to get home. Next, they saw the police beating one of the dealers. The cops demanded that the suspects spill some info. One of them eventually did, revealing the location of their stash. So the couple went with the police to find it. There were five hundred kilos of marijuana hidden in potato sacks. "That's a huge pile," Jewel said. "Anyway, we helped them load these sacks on the *federales'* boat so they could take the drugs back. After this five-hour ordeal, they gave both Steve and me a handful of pot, which we passed on to the cook at the 'resort.' The cook insisted that she needed it for her arthritis."

Jewel swears it's true.

But Steve and Jewel's relationship wasn't just fun and games. "Next thing I know, we started writing songs together," Poltz told *People* magazine. One of those songs was "You Were Meant for Me," which they wrote together during an afternoon in Mexico. (They wrote "Adrian" together, too.) And Steve was the one who brought Jewel up to par with the rest of the world when it came to pop culture. At nineteen, Jewel had never heard of the Beatles' *White Album* and she still had no clue who the Replacements were. "Steve sat me down and had what he called Jewel 101 classes," she said fondly of him. He was really interested in molding Jewel into a better all-around musician, which meant she had some learning to do.

Steve said that he made it his duty to bring Jewel into the MTV generation. She was so out of it, pop-musically. "Once I was with her, and 'I Want to Hold Your Hand' came on the radio. She said, 'Now, what's this band called? Is this the Stones?' And she was deadly serious. I said, 'This is the Beatles.' She was like, 'Oh! I like it.'" He'd put on albums and stuff he had at home just so she'd know what was out there. After all, there are a lot of musical greats besides Ella Fitzgerald and Cole Porter.

Jewel loved learning, even if she didn't exactly love Steve, not *that* way, anyway. Steve just wasn't meant for Jewel, so they eventually broke up. Don't worry, they've stayed very close ever since their romantic days back in San Diego. Neither of them says it's even the slightest bit weird to hang with an ex. "He's the only person who, when he sings, makes me cry," she admitted. He replied, "There is just a cool chemistry that we have. It's nice."

The exes still work together musically and hang out as friends. "We just dig each other a lot. We write incredible songs together. It makes me get goosebumps," she said. Jewel chose Steve to be her steamy love interest in the "You Were Meant for Me" video that's on VH1 and MTV. (Yep, that's him.) Jewel collaborated with Steve on his solo debut album, called *One Left Shoe*. They sing duets on three of the songs, and she cowrote one of them.

Back to San Diego—when Jewel first started seeing Steve, she was on the way to being happy again. Oh, but there was still that one little thing she had to worry about: money. She *really* started talking it over with her mother. After all, Nedra was the reason Jewel had come to San Diego (well, San Diego had been a blast over spring break from Interlochen). Jewel thought that her mother could figure things out with her. She always seemed to know what was right for her daughter, not only because she gave birth to her but also because they were best friends. Jewel asked Nedra questions like "What is this?" and "Why am I so unhappy?" Jewel would say, "I don't know how to do anything." Jewel admits that she wasn't the sweetest person in the world while she was going through her very early midlife crisis. She respected the advice her mother gave her. Nedra told Jewel, "Stop hiding." When Jewel sat down to think about her life in San Diego, she realized she had been hiding from herself. She had tried to get in with a crowd of rich kids, she had tried to be a really good waitress and stick to it, but none of that had worked.

About that time, Nedra's father, Jewel's other grandfather, died. Just when Jewel's need for a really big and important change was coming to a head, her mother had to leave. To make matters even worse, Jewel couldn't go because they, once again, had no money. Before Nedra left, she said to Jewel, for the forty-billionth time, "You have to figure out what your spirit wants. You do have a spirit, and it does have a purpose." Jewel's mother planted the seed in her daughter's brain that helped her to realize her endless possibilities.

Jewel called her mom in Alaska. According to Nedra, Jewel told her, "This [music] industry, it's so hard to make it. You should always have a plan B." Nedra's response? "Forget plan B, never have a plan B. If you have a fallback plan, you'll fall back. I want to hear what plan A is; I don't want to know about plan B." That was the conversation as Nedra told it to *Interview* magazine. Here's the rest.

Jewel called her back soon after that, and she said, "I know what plan A is. I *need* to do this music thing. I was afraid. What if I really go for it and fail? I wonder how I would ever face my life. Then I realized I *have* to do it. It's the only choice I have."

Nedra's response, as told to *Interview:* "That is the most important information you have for yourself. Now tell me why you have no choice. To know your own intent is what will support your dream. You're going to need to reference it again and again. You're going to have to remember why you needed to do it when you're discouraged."

Jewel explained to her mother that she wanted to make a difference in lives, in little ways and big ways.

"I was a terrible waitress, I was a terrible retail salesperson. So I said to myself, 'Do it or die,'" Jewel explained. Those are all the reasons she quit her job. She was willing to pull herself out of society in order to follow her dreams. Also, she had the support of the people closest to her—her mom and Steve (whom she was still dating). She was ready. She quit her last job and sold her old, beat-up Datsun. She borrowed money from a friend—she didn't need much. "So I moved into my van—and I did it." A blue '79 VW van became her home. Jewel was delighted.

The whole thing was actually her mom's idea. When Nedra suggested it, Jewel was for it right away. She understood what her mom was thinking. Nedra was trying to help Jewel make her dreams match her needs. If Jewel could rid herself of major bills, like, say, rent, she wouldn't need to work unsatisfying service jobs. She wouldn't need much money—only a bare minimum to survive. Then all Jewel had to do was live day to day, singing, writing, and living her music. Believe it or not, when Nedra returned from Alaska, she decided to do the same thing. As dramatic as it sounds, it's totally true. Mom and daughter lived side by side, in their respective vans.

In one of Jewel's explanations of this move, she said, "It's amazing what happens when you focus your brain on something. I think the hardest part is figuring out what you want to do. Kids aren't asked what makes us happy, but

(Steve Labadessa/Outline)

When Jewel started out, she was living out of her van in San Diego. But her debut album, *Pieces of You,* went on to sell over eight million copies.

Jewel rocks
out at a live
performance on
her 1997 tour.
(Todd Kaplan/ Star File)

At the 1997 Grammy Awards, Jewel sparkles.

(Gerardo Somoza / Outline)

When Jewel goes out, she's never without a date. Whether it's her then boyfriend, Michel (left), at the 1997 MTV Music Awards or her brother, Atz (below).

(John Spelmann / Retna Ltd.)

A girl and her guitar. Jewel's been
performing since she was six years old.

Jewel, Sheryl Crow, and Shawn Colvin. Three of the most popular performers at the 1997 Lilith Fair pose for a picture.

Singer, songwriter, actress— and even supermodel!

(Guy Aroch / Retna Ltd.)

(Guy Aroch / Retna Ltd.)

(Norman Ng for Baskin / Outline)

Jewel is one of the most influential songwriters of her generation.

rather how we're going to earn a living. So our passions become our hobbies. Everyone fuels themselves enough to keep going—to keep believing—but never more than that. People don't ever fan the flame." This was not going to happen to her. Even though she was raised singing, she had never considered it a career option. "I never thought I could make a living at it. But it was the one thing that made me really, really happy, so I decided to go for it." Jewel's passion was destined to become much more than a hobby.

7

Rising Horizons

It worked. It was like overnight that Jewel discovered happiness while riding around in a VW van. She was finally the one choosing and controlling her own destiny. In those early months of 1993, Jewel and Nedra no longer had their apartments, but life was twenty times better. "Instead of focusing on what I didn't have, I would focus on what I wanted," Jewel said. As for Nedra, she was just happy to see the transformation in her daughter. "I watched her with a lot of delight," she said. The mother-daughter pair, bonded by a love for following Jewel's dreams, often traveled together in their vans. "I sensed that if singing is what she attached to her passion, then she'd have what it takes," Nedra added.

What was the dream? It wasn't about fame,

fortune, or playing the guitar on MTV. It definitely wasn't about scoring record deals and graduating from gigs to sold-out shows. To Jewel, hopping into that van and singing to whoever would listen was what it was about. She did it to earn a little cash, not to make millions. Here's how she explained her motives: "I just prayed in my van every night that by me living my dream somehow people would remember theirs." She wanted to fill her life with purpose—a purpose that made her feel fulfilled and content—and she hoped that she could inspire other people to do the same with their lives. *"That* is very beautiful," she said.

So the mother-daughter team hit the road. "We chose sites, parked together, opened our doors, and had tea," Nedra said. They both had their favorite parking spots. Nedra liked to park by the ocean. Jewel chose a small tree that blossomed year-round. She liked to nudge her van next to the tree and open her window so flowers would spill into her small living quarters. Living in an old VW might seem unappealing to most people, but to Jewel it was home. Of course, most people didn't grow up without electricity and running water—so maybe Jewel had an advantage—she knew what life was like without amenities. (In one interview, she explained it like this: "Running water? It was, like, who cares . . .") Anyway, she found her van life very liberating and didn't miss the luxuries of apartment life—like a shower, TV, and microwave. "I was already living on very little [in the apartment], and it wasn't difficult to live in my van."

With a little help and a lot of encouragement from her boyfriend Steve, Jewel got a weekly Thursday night gig at a little coffee shop called the Innerchange in nearby Pacific Beach. That helped pay her minimal expenses. And she loved it.

Her first solo performances were big disappointments. Right before her big debut, Jewel spent most of the day handing out flyers to promote her act. She was excited and thought she had made enough of an impression on people to generate an audience. But that night, only six people showed up. She had to leave the stage because she was so heartbroken. She went around the back and cried. Jewel was used to performing in front of large groups, and that night's audience could hardly be considered a group—a handful, maybe. Jewel got herself together and worked the tiny audience to her advantage. Instead of being totally down about the turnout, she transformed her show into a very intimate, musical experience between the listeners and herself. She created six new fans. They told their friends about the emotional, sincere folk singer, and she drew more and more listeners each week from then on. She vowed never to hand out flyers again, since it did absolutely no good and only led to frustration. She relied on word-of-mouth. Fans became the ultimate measure of Jewel's success.

Nancy Porter, owner of the now-defunct Innerchange, was never disappointed in Jewel. From the first time she met her, she was impressed. "She had just gotten into town, and at the time she was really rough," Porter said. She told Jewel she could have Thursday nights, but she would have to get her name out on her own. The Innerchange wasn't into advertising for performers. Even though there were only a few people for the first few shows, Porter believed in her. "I was new, too. But I could see she had the talent, and she really disciplined herself and kept at it. You could just tell she would succeed." Jewel was eventually very good for business, and Porter was pleased, even surprised by the degree of success that Jewel, a complete unknown, achieved.

The Innerchange only took up four to five hours a week of Jewel's time—there were 168 more hours to kill. During the rest of the week, Jewel spent her days playing music for tourists and the San Diego boardwalk regulars. She relied on them for the tiny bit of money she needed to buy gas and food. She was very happy to be relying on the "random kindness of so many strangers" in order to sustain her nomadic way of life. At least this way, Jewel only depended on herself—and her music. To her, that was living. As she put it, "I was drunk on life." Her days consisted of lots of surfing and writing. She loved the freedom and wildness of the ocean, the roar of the waves. To her, riding the waves was like taming an unbroken horse. She also had the freedom and inspired mindset that was conducive to writing. Despite everything she'd been through, Jewel wrote hundreds of optimistic, sweet songs during this period. She always carried around a notebook to write down thoughts that later could become lyrics.

There wasn't a whole lot to do, but Jewel managed to have a good life with what she had—a surfboard, a backpack, a mattress, and a few books that she'd read at night by candlelight. That was pretty much it. She was spending a lot of her alone time creating herself. "In silence you hear who you're going to become. It was really a time that taught me a lot about faith."

Despite her ever-present lack of cash to buy healthy foods, she was feeling better kidneywise—at least a little bit. She read a lot of scientific books to learn about what was going on in her body. Overall, her outlook on life greatly improved, and she stopped being depressed. Therefore, her body was healthier, too—even though she could afford to eat only peanut butter sandwiches and carrots. Oh, and a few fruits from the bountiful California orchards—she'd pick them on the side of the road and quickly drive away in her van. Jewel and Nedra also visited local bars for happy hour—which usually had a large variety of yummy snacks. Sometimes people would even help Jewel out. They'd hear her story and be moved by this beautiful, talented teenager. During her shows at the Innerchange, she'd say, "Angels, or whoever, I really need a place to shower." Someone would usually accept this call of duty and offer their services. One guy eventually gave Jewel the keys to his apartment and let her take showers before her Thursday night shows. It was obvious that he was interested in her, but Jewel said, "I was clear that I wasn't available." He was nice to her all the same. Lord knows, Jewel could take care of herself if she needed to.

The showers were great, but obviously Jewel needed water more than once a week. She'd go to public restrooms to clean herself up or get a drink—like at the Denny's or Kmart, by the intersection of Mission and Gabriel streets in San Diego. Jewel would wash her hair in the sinks there sometimes. She would be quite hurt when people around her whispered catty remarks about the homeless. Oh, well, there weren't many down sides for Jewel and life in her van, so she could live with that one.

Very quickly, Jewel started going places, even though she didn't think so.

By Jewel's own admission, she wasn't a very good guitar player. How could she be? She had just started learning at Interlochen less than a year before. She didn't think her cutesy little coffee shop songs were groundbreaking. If anything, Jewel considered herself a novice. Someone who, if given some time and a chance, could be great.

Her fans in San Diego didn't agree. In less than five months, Jewel had gone from putting on a show that drew a six-person crowd to packing the Innerchange so full that local Jewel junkies were spilling out onto the street just to catch a glimpse of her. Word had gotten around. She was even written up in a local San Diego music 'zine. The reviewer went on and on about this awesome teenage singer who sang in a coffee shop, some incredible young woman named Jewel Kilcher. After that, even more people flocked to the Innerchange on Thursday nights.

Her music was basic and simple, and "it touched you inside," said one of her first fans, Soo Hom, who didn't miss a show. "I thought she was absolutely incredible," he added. Those days, it was just Jewel and a guitar that she carried onstage herself. She was very raw and very honest. At that time Jewel was just learning how to handle crowds. She was growing as a performer and working to perfect her stage presence.

Back then, Jewel would sit down on a stage stool and chat with the audience. She'd tell stories of her life in Homer and her adventures in Mexico. "She seemed like somebody next door telling you about her life," Hom said. To these audiences, Jewel was a real girl struggling to make money by making music, which she was great at. She endeared herself to her audiences with her idiosyncrasies, her forgetfulness. Her lapses made her easy to relate to. She'd forget guitar picks and would borrow them from the audience or from the other bands playing that night. Jewel was a joker, too. If someone tried to leave during a show, Jewel, in true spunky Jewel style, would stop singing and ask the person, "Hey, are you leaving?" Then she'd say, "Well, let's all tell him good-bye." Then, when the show was over, she had a favorite tradition. Jewel would rush to the door to catch her fans before they left. She wanted to shake hands with all the fans who had come to see her and sincerely thank them for being there. In these little ways, Jewel bonded with her audiences. She made them laugh at her antics and stories, and she made them cry with her music.

Fans were the most important thing to Jewel. She had picked that belief up from her father. He was the one who taught her to be responsive and always to be her best onstage. After all, if people were paying, you had to live up to their high expectations. So, like Atz, she did everything she could to charm her audiences. Jewel's father didn't believe in writing a set list, which is a list of songs to perform. Set lists make performers' lives easier because they can anticipate and perfect their acts. But those kinds of lists also can make the performances a bit impersonal. So Jewel never writes set lists, even at her bigger gigs, like those today. Instead, she always tries to sing what will please each audience. "You have to read the crowd's mood," she said.

Another San Diego singer, Joy Eden Harrison, was so impressed by Jewel's stage presence that she tried not to miss a performance. Joy, one of Jewel's closest California friends, watched Jewel at the Innerchange in complete awe because crowds loved Jewel. They loved her because she was their servant and because she invited them into her heart. "Any love the audience gave Jewel got sent right back to them—with Jewel, it's a continuous cycle," Harrison said. Jewel was always open and available to her crowd. Harrison added, "When Jewel's onstage, she comes from a place of love and service and giving."

Eventually, the Innerchange became so crowded that Jewel had to maneuver her way across the tops of tables just to get to the stage. Hom said that one time she grabbed his shoulder for support, to keep from falling. Even before she became a superstar, he was touched. "My left shoulder is special," he joked. "Not many people get to help out Jewel."

Jewel loved her Innerchange audience— people like Soo. "They were an amazing audience, from ages eight to eighty. That's what I want my fan base to be," she said. She was completely on target, as if she'd predicted the future. Folks of all ages are into Jewel.

She was living her dream—finally. And she made some great friends along the way, like Joy, who met Jewel after a show. They got to talking and became close friends who were extremely supportive of each other's career. A lot of the singers in the San Diego scene started hanging out with Jewel. People like Cindy Lee Berryhill, Elizabeth Hummel, and Joy, all of whom are still in California performing. Joy said, "We had these dinner parties where we would all sit around and talk about life and music. Then we'd pull out our guitars and play for each other. I heard 'You Were Meant for Me' right after she wrote it. I loved it." Jewel wasn't able to attend many of the dinners. She just got too busy. With her success at the Innerchange came new and bigger gigs. She started playing at nearby coffee shops that were larger and could hold bigger crowds. She even got to sing at Java Joe's, the place that had once fired her for being a bad waitress.

Jewel Kilcher's name was being buzzed all over San Diego as she kept gaining popularity. At this point, she'd been pursuing her dream for about five months, and she'd been living in her VW van for the same amount of time. Life was about to change for Jewel once again. What was about to happen would be a total shock to her. Her career was about to get the huge jump start it needed. Record company big wigs from L.A. began driving down to sleepy little San Diego to check out the hot coffee shop diva from Alaska.

8

Making Records

"**I** could hardly believe it when the first person asked if I wanted to make a record. I asked if they were kidding, since I was only at this thing for five months," Jewel said. But the record company people were on a mission—a mission to sign Jewel up and make her a star. It was real. They were there to see Jewel Kilcher.

Her fans were just as pleased as Jewel. Their reaction wasn't surprising since they were the ones who had discovered her and made her who she was in San Diego. If the Jewel junkies hadn't been so enthusiastic about her, the record companies would never have expressed interest. "You can't imagine the pride of my fans. It was like, you know, I was everybody's daughter, everybody's sister, and they were happy for me," she said. When the record people started coming to the Innerchange, the owner, Nancy Porter, was extremely excited. She showed her support for Jewel by putting signs up all over the shop that read, "Welcome Warner Brothers Music" and things like that.

When the record representatives arrived, Jewel's fans pounced on them to rave about her. The music reps were not allowed to leave the coffeehouse without hearing earfuls of admiration for Jewel from her faithful followers. "They were so supportive—really dear," she said of her fans.

Jewel was happy but skeptical, "I was really scared to go into the business because you hear all these horror stories." Record people who are trying to strike up a deal aren't known for their honesty and sincerity, and Jewel was no fool. She was very picky about whom she would work with on something as personal and important to her as her music—her life's passion.

At the same time that the music companies were nosing around, Jewel had all of these artist and repertoire representatives (called A&R reps) making her offers. Good offers. It was an exciting but complicated time for Jewel. She didn't know anyone in the business and was actually quite confused. Here's how Jewel explained it: "I was scared because I was just playing guitar for such a little time. Creatively, I was very tender and young—like grass. If you have a lawn and you walk on it too much, it dies. But if you don't nurture it enough, it dies as well. It's a real fine line. I was really afraid of being trampled on, but I also wanted to be nurtured and supported."

A woman named Inga Vainshtein, a Russian-born former movie exec, was the person with whom Jewel clicked first. She was the one A&R rep Jewel really liked and trusted. Inga guided Jewel through the mass of corporate attention she was getting. Later, Inga became Jewel's co-manager along with Nedra (the two women shared that job until February 1998, when Nedra started managing her daughter by herself). Inga said, "The first time I saw Jewel perform, she reminded me of Barbra Streisand meets Meryl Streep." She told Atlantic's Jenny Price about San Diego's diamond in the rough. Price decided to come take a look at Jewel for herself.

"My response to hearing her was: Wow! My mouth was hanging open. It was something very special," Price said. Atlantic Records ended up giving Jewel the best feeling. Even though lots of record companies were flying her to New York and wooing her with money deals, Jewel decided to stick with Atlantic. Their deal was great. More important, the people, including Price, were warm and sincere and believed in Jewel being Jewel. Atlantic wasn't out to change her sound or make her into something different, something more media-savvy. Jewel signed with them, a good move on her part. Atlantic was in love with Jewel, and the company stayed true to its promises. The company was going to support and promote Jewel through thick and thin, until she and her songs became popular.

Besides, Danny Goldberg, who was then president of Atlantic Records, wooed her with his soulful and spiritual words. He was supportive, and she liked that. Plus, he told Jewel that he thought the next Bob Dylan would be a woman. With a laugh, Jewel said, "And even if that's not true, it's what every singer-songwriter wants to hear." When Jewel closed the deal by signing on the dotted line, she dropped her last name. It was Atlantic's suggestion. From then on, Jewel Kilcher would simply be known musically as Jewel.

Another plus to signing with Atlantic was producer Ben Keith. A producer is the person who oversees an artist's recording session, guiding singers from beginning to end. That person can also shape and mold the artist's music, which can be a problem if the artist doesn't agree with the producer's vision for the album. Unfortunately, that happens a lot. Jewel wanted to avoid that situation at all costs. "My first concern is how I would exist in this business and remain true. I was looking for the producer who wouldn't produce me," Jewel said. That's why she chose Ben Keith, whose résumé included producing legendary acts like Neil Young and some music for James Taylor. Jewel told *Interview* in July 1997, "I had met with a lot of them, and they all wanted to take me to the potential of what I could be in a couple of years. I was looking for somebody who would let me at least be who I was, so I could be honest and recognizable to myself and my fans. I chose Ben Keith for those reasons."

Ben was the man who wouldn't trample Jewel. She said, if nothing else, *Pieces of You* is very honest. It is totally representative of the singer and where she was musically in 1994 when she recorded it. "In some ways, I wish it had a little more direction, but I really don't," she admitted. Sometimes the album makes Jewel cry, because she wishes it was better. But at the same time, she's glad that it's *her*. "I was a girl who sang in coffeehouses—that's what you get on the record."

Remaining true to herself, Jewel recorded ten songs for her first album in a coffeehouse—at the Innerchange, to be exact. It was important to Jewel to record the songs there, though it was unusual for a signed artist not to sing in a studio. Jenny Price said, "We just thought that since she started out in San Diego, it would be nice to have her record right down there at the little club she started at. It's more genuine, and it's appropriate for her." Jewel was relieved and happy when she heard the decision. To her, the Innerchange was home, and she loved the thought of recording in front of the people who had made the whole thing happen—her faithful San Diego fans. "I feel so comfortable here," Jewel told the *San Diego Union-Tribune* right before the big day. "I can give a better performance here than in a studio." Much of what later became a breakthrough album called *Pieces of You* was recorded July 21 and 22, 1994, on a Thursday and a Friday night. Fans filled the rooms to watch. Tickets were just eight dollars and were sold on a first-come, first-served basis.

The rest of Jewel's album, which turned out to be five songs, was recorded in an equally intimate setting. She was asked to go to Neil Young's Half Moon Bay Ranch in Northern California. She was ecstatic to be there and a little amazed. It was a huge compliment to her talent just to record on the ranch of a legend. Ben Keith was there, of course, and so were veteran band members Kenny Butrey, Tim

Drummond, and Spooner Oldham, all members of Young's band the Stray Gators. Jewel said, "It was an overwhelming experience to have Bob Dylan's drummer . . . Janis Joplin's organ player." You can't find more experienced musicians. Jewel loved working with them. They would say things to her like, "We play for you—not the record companies, managers, or producers. You tell us what *you* want."

What she wanted was an album that looked at her world and what she was doing at that time in her life. "I want to capture the rawness of it," she said. "I can do a serious, more polished album next time."

Pieces of You was released in February 1995. She was only nineteen years old. She'd just been playing the guitar for a year and a half, and she hadn't been writing songs for much longer than that. It was all very unreal to Jewel.

Her life changed dramatically, too. Obviously, Jewel was able to move out of her van and back into a real building. She no longer needed to worry about overhead or how she was going to pay for her peanut butter and carrots. In fact, she got to upgrade to healthier, mostly vegetarian food. Spending money was still hard. Even with the advance money Jewel got, she couldn't get used to the thought that it could all be over the next day, and she could be poor again. That's how it is for Jewel, a girl who had to pinch pennies all her life. Just to have five dollars in her pocket was happiness and safety. Now, she was able to buy an entire house.

Even in those days, right after the whirlwind of getting signed, Jewel was never too busy for her friends. Joy remembers those days with Jewel well. Jewel still made time to offer Joy advice and encouragement. "When I was going through hard times, she was the person that I loved to talk to," Joy said. Just a twenty-minute phone call with Jewel, and Joy felt tons better. Even when Joy couldn't get through to Jewel, she got a lift just hearing Jewel's cool answering-machine messages. There was always a poem or a really creative spontaneous song. The one Joy remembers most was a blues tune with Jewel singing about her cold and runny nose.

Joy called her for important things, too. "She's so insightful about life, she had a real clarity of vision." Jewel always reminded Joy to appreciate her own worth and never compromise it. "Like if a place offers you a gig for ten dollars, you don't take it, and you don't agonize about it. Not when you're worth a lot more than that," Jewel told Joy. Jewel would say to Joy, "It's not that you're worth more than others, but you have to respect yourself and realize there's room for everybody." Jewel also talked about how Joy had to follow her dreams. "Jewel said those things to me in a small town, but she's carried the same message with her in her tremendous success," Joy said.

The two friends also spent some time together writing songs. Joy was trying to finish a song called "Angel Town," and Jewel was more than happy to help her. Joy said they had fun being serious, but they also had a great time being goofy, just like good girlfriends.

That's really what Jewel was and still is to Joy. "A lovely thing Jewel did—she invited me onstage at one of her crowded gigs." It was an especially supportive thing for Jewel to do since a big-shot record producer was coming to hear Joy's show a few nights later. After singing a few songs to Jewel's audience, Joy could also ask the crowd to come to her gig in a few days. That way, Joy's performance would be filled with people when the record company guy came to see her. "It gave me exposure at a time when I really needed it. That was a caretaking, friend thing to do," Joy said.

9

On Tour

An album meant a tour, and Jewel had to embark on her first because it was time to sell *Pieces of You*. It needed its star's effervescent stage presence to promote it; an album, any album, can't do justice to Jewel's voice and overall appeal. Only this time, touring didn't mean traveling from town to town, as it once did in Homer, at Interlochen, or in Southern California. Jewel's job was to travel nationwide on Atlantic's money. She had conquered small towns; now she was sent out to endear herself to audiences on a much larger scale.

Jewel admits that it was scary, even though she knew she could handle it—along with whatever else her career required of her. In June 1995, when she was just embarking on her tour, Jewel confessed that she—yes, she—was insecure, but just about her guitar abilities. "My hands are young when it comes to the guitar. They can't do what my head hears. Right now, I'm much more loyal to my poetry. With words, I'm more comfortable." She went out on the road before she'd even mastered the guitar, carrying notebooks so she could scribble down her poems. Despite her awkward fingers, Jewel said, "I feel most myself when I'm onstage, when I'm singing or when I'm writing. It's just in my blood." Jewel was happy to have the chance to make those big and little changes in people's lives through her musical influence. That was her dream—it wasn't about money and fame. Music was the way Jewel could spread her optimistic ideas. At the same time she said, "I got into this versus other arts because it's one of the last, real living art forms that still has a big influence. A lot of the other arts are too easily intellectualized." Her catchy tunes had big messages. Jewel liked the fact that she was able to deliver them minus a textbook. With that realization, she was ready to sing her heart out.

Good thing, too—touring was hardcore because it was absolutely nonstop. It was nothing for Jewel to do forty shows in thirty days. Also, she had to keep that same schedule for more than two years, though she didn't know that when she started. Atlantic was devoted to making her album work—no matter how long she had to stay on the road. The first release off *Pieces of You* was "Who Will Save Your Soul." Even though folk songs like that weren't getting airplay at the time (February 1995 was a grunge year—artists like Pearl Jam and Stone Temple Pilots topped the charts), Atlantic pushed Jewel's act anyway. The company even had a memo circulating through its offices that Jewel had to be booked for every free second she had. If her time wasn't filled, every department in the company was supposed to get on it immediately. As a result, her schedule was tough. It wasn't unusual for Jewel to wake up and do live radio show interviews in the morning, a local newspaper and/or television spot in the afternoon, a night performance, and then a late coffeehouse gig in the evening to end her hectic day.

Atlantic teamed Jewel with other acts on the label. They basically stuck the nineteen-year-old with anyone who would take her. So she opened for bands like the Ramones, Everclear, and even goth king Peter Murphy. It was the company's attempt to get her name out and to win people over—even if the manly, noisy acts were total night-and-day from Jewel's softer, soulful act. Touring wasn't easy for Jewel. Sometimes she was even booed offstage, especially by heavy-metal Murphy fans. That obviously didn't work so well. Neither did a spot

Atlantic booked for Jewel in a Detroit inner-city high school. Excited students thought they were about to see Death Row Records rap act Jewell (pronounced "joo-ELLE") and were really disappointed and rude when Jewel, a folk girl with her guitar, started singing on their stage. "By the end, the auditorium was almost empty," Jewel said.

Next, Jewel was paired with alternative acts like Belly and Catherine Wheel, both of which were better matches for Jewel. Even those fans weren't super-receptive to Jewel's musical style, which was very organic and simple. Jewel was way more "Me and a Gun" by Tori Amos than "Feed the Tree" by Belly.

Another strategy—the one that worked the best—was when Jewel hit the road by herself. This was an ingenious attempt at building "little Jewel fan bases" all over the country. It worked when Jewel stuck to a schedule that went something like this: Monday nights she performed in Toronto, Wednesdays in Chicago, Thursdays in Detroit, Saturdays in Ohio, and back to Toronto for another Monday show. That's how she started winning people over, one city at a time, with repeat performances and venues. She created close relationships and ties to each of those cities.

Here's the kind of show she did at these smaller, regional venues, as she told *Now* magazine in June 1995: "I usually start with something upbeat like 'Race Car Driver' (a sweet, funny song that didn't make *POY*) to get people's wit going and then move them into some more serious songs. After that, maybe a song called 'God's Gift to Women,' the one that goes with the hitchhiking story. Sometimes I tell that story, sometimes I don't, depending on the crowd (remember, the one about keeping a knife in her boot?). Some audiences need to be drawn in a little more. Then I can throw in a pretty one like 'Angel Standing By' and end with the yodel. I used to begin with the yodel to get people's attention, but I found it was a hard act to follow." Of course, the story about Steve Poltz and Jewel with the Mexican *federales* comes up often, too, during Jewel's performances.

Slowly, small groups of fans started to respond. Jewel won them over one by one, show after show. She said, "I made them into guerrillas of my music." She knew if people would just listen and give her a chance, they might actually like her and her music. But gaining any kind of respect was hard, especially in 1995, when "chick" music was dominated by Joan Osborne and Tori Amos. Radio stations insisted that in the age of grunge, there just wasn't room for another woman on the airwaves, especially not a folk singer. Jewel struggled to get noticed on a nationwide scale.

She worked hard to keep her spirits up. All she had to do was think back to her struggling days of working. "A day of long interviews and bad shows is better than one hour of waitressing. I feel blessed to be doing what I love." She wasn't complaining; she never did, no matter how hard her schedule became. An Atlantic rep said, "She worked seven days a week and never let us down. Never, never, never. She will work as hard as a human being can physically work."

Instead of moaning about her lack of sleep—sometimes she had only three hours to rest between her late-night and early-morning engagements—Jewel used her precious energy to talk about the happy things in her life. She told a reporter in June 1995 about one of her fans who was able to put Jewel's whole life into perspective with a few introspective words to her. The fan, a forty-year-old man, came up to Jewel after one of her performances to tell her that he'd given up his hobby of writing poetry a few years before—he just didn't believe in it anymore, nor did he have the heart. He went on to explain that Jewel and her wonderful music were the inspiration he needed to take it up again. He went to another Jewel show the next time she performed in his area—this time, he talked to Jewel again and showed her his newly written poems. Jewel said, "That is what makes it all worthwhile. The fact that I can touch someone and help them rekindle their dreams."

Pieces of You wasn't exactly flying off the shelves. But Jewel wasn't surprised or disappointed. She had her handful of fans, and she was thrilled with them. "As I predicted, nothing big happened. Radio stations said they would play [*Pieces of You*] only over their dead bodies. That was fine with me. I didn't think I'd exist within what was popular." Along those same lines, Jewel's new album was heading in the direction that she and her record company expected. Atlantic only planned on selling fifty thousand copies of the album in the first place. Then they expected her to go into the studio and start working on her second effort. (Eventually, Jewel blew Atlantic away by selling a whopping eight-million-plus units.) But at that time, in 1995, *Pieces of You* was far from big, and it basically collected dust on record shop shelves across America. *Pieces of You* wasn't a disappointment, really, but it definitely wasn't a moneymaker, either.

Radio stations were impossible. They didn't help matters—Jewel needed them to play her music, if not for herself, then for her record company, which had been so diligently backing her. Stations flatly refused. Even with Atlantic's prodding, the airways wouldn't touch her. She was a pop-folk act tinged with a tiny bit of country. She didn't fit a 1995 alternative radio mold. Instead, Jewel was the kind of act that stations avoided more than Michael Jackson. She tried to fight feeling bad about it, but even optimistic Jewel realized that the total lack of radio support was causing quite a struggle for *Pieces of You.*

Critics weren't helping, either. As far as they were concerned, Jewel was a nineteen-year-old, half-baked Alaskan ditz who wanted people to listen to her silly little record with sugary lyrics like "I'm sensitive and I'd like to stay that way." Come on, was this chick for real? They didn't buy her story, literally. Growing up on a Homer homestead, canning salmon, and hitching to school . . . singing her heart out from her VW van traveling apartment while surviving on peanut butter and carrots. Nobody—besides the fans and record company who loved her— could swallow it. And then she went on about her philosophical ideas—blah, blah, blah.

Many of the criticisms were really *that* harsh. One writer's opinion: "Jewel is convincing enough when she sticks to catchy love songs and doesn't take on social injustice head-on or try to paint bohemian, Dylanesque tableaux. Time to recalibrate that cheese alert, perhaps." Another put it a little nicer. She accused Jewel of saying all kinds of naive, socially conscious stuff that most people only write in their diaries.

Jewel didn't go unscathed by their biting words. Sometimes she cried when she listened to her own CD. Caving into her critics' harshest words, she couldn't believe how "dorky" it sounded. When people said Jewel wrote songs that sounded like a woeful teenage girl's journal scribblings, she would answer, "I wrote the songs when I was seventeen!" Jeez, some people just don't get it. "These writers put in the papers, 'She's naive,' as though it were some discovery. And, like, I'm young! It's no big discovery." Eventually, Jewel learned to deal. She laughed at the negative comments a little more; she took them a little less seriously. She came to the conclusion that what she was doing, her music, was very pure. People can tear it apart, dissect it, and label it, but, "Whatever. Who really cares, anyway? I'm just a person trying to figure out her life." It took a few years in the public spotlight before Jewel *really* figured it out. Now, when she describes herself, she says she's naive but wise. Very girlish but womanly. Very spiritual but real. Very sweet, but she cusses, and those are all things that change and grow. She explained, "I enjoy being all of those things for people onstage because it's not often we get to see that . . . it brings freedom into people's lives."

Atlantic believed in Jewel, even when the nineteen-year-old understandably questioned herself. This kind of devotion to an act was unusual. It's protocol for a record company to release an album, then get busy calculating the artist's sales, concert receipts, radio and video airplay. With those numbers, companies like Atlantic can figure out whether they have a hit on their hands. If they don't, they often turn their attention and money to another artist who has a better shot of becoming big. Jewel's numbers weren't exactly adding up. Even though "Who Will Save Your Soul" hadn't hit a single chart, Atlantic stuck behind their wavering star. Likewise, *Pieces of You* hadn't become a *Billboard* regular, either.

"At a lot of companies, Jewel would have been over a long time ago," explained Ron Shapiro, Atlantic's senior vice president and general manager when *Pieces of You* was released. "But the moment I met her and saw her live, I knew she was one of a kind and we had to try." They did—spurred by the amazing response to their nineteen-year-old discovery.

Even if people didn't buy the record, didn't get what Jewel was all about, and didn't think that *Pieces of You* was anything but a stylistic mess, they couldn't deny what they saw when Jewel was onstage. That's where she truly shone. She told witty and amazing personal stories; she was completely down-to-earth and connected to her audiences; she did wonderfully humorous impersonations (she's famous for her imitation of the Cranberries' Dolores O'Riordan); and she had that show-stopping gimmick of yodeling. Her crowds couldn't resist. So Atlantic set out to make those crowds even bigger. If nothing else, "You can't deny what she does. . . . She has one of the most God-given voices I have ever heard an artist be given," Shapiro added.

Jewel's voice was the hand grenade, her personality the pin. Jewel would trill like a little girl (like in "Adrian"), croon like Joan Baez ("Who Will Save Your Soul"), then belt out like Billie Holiday ("Angel Standing By"), only she could do it all in the span of a single song ("Foolish Games") and make it all believable. Jewel live was an amazing treat, and she only improved with the practice that accompanies relentless touring.

Now you know why Atlantic stuck around. Jewel's *Pieces of You* has an important claim to fame around the Atlantic offices today. It took the longest amount of time to break in the company's history—fourteen months, to be exact—and it also required more work and devotion than they'd ever put into a single artist.

10

Breaking Out

When *Pieces of You* floundered because industry big wigs, local radio stations, and MTV refused to play it, Jewel decided she'd have to change their minds once and for all. She told herself, "I'm gonna tour my brains out to prove you all wrong." Her strategy worked. Finally, after a lot of brain and brawn, Jewel's sleepy little album started to break. There were a lot of reasons. Innocently enough, Jewel did a radio show called "All Things Considered" on National Public Radio. The spot aired in August 1995. By a total fluke, a man named Darrell Larson happened to catch Jewel's interview and a few of her songs. He hadn't seen her or even heard of Jewel, but he was blinded by what he heard.

Larson was working on a benefit show for the

Children's Defense Fund, a rock-opera version of *The Wizard of Oz*. Larson went to the show's producer, Jonathan Brauer, and asked him to get a copy of Jewel's album and give it a listen. Brauer ignored Larson; he'd never even heard of this girl. Larson got his way, though, and Brauer was convinced. In September 1995, Jewel got a call and eagerly signed on to the program. She really didn't know much about it, but she knew the production was first class. Other stars committed to the project were The Who's Roger Daltrey, singing legends Carly Simon, David Sanborn, Natalie Cole, and Jackson Browne. Even actors like Debra Winger and Alfre Woodard were participating. Yep, for Jewel, this was the chance of a lifetime.

Jewel didn't know much about the classic Judy Garland movie. "I think I saw it once as a kid." That didn't matter, she knew she had to go for this one. The producers knew she wasn't an experienced actress (not yet, anyway—now she has a movie called *Ride with the Devil*), and they asked if that bothered her. Her answer: "Um, no. I've already memorized my lines." It may have been her first time acting professionally, but it certainly wasn't her first time at Lincoln Center—she had gotten that experience out of the way in high school. Finally, some of the acting that she had picked up and perfected at Interlochen would be put to use. That was the real highlight for Jewel, because she was itching to use a different part of herself, a different talent—that's why she'd spent all that cash to go to Interlochen. "So to be able to accept the challenge and the complete scare—and being the lead role of these big people? I mean, what right do I have to be there? I'd oscillate between 'I'm an idiot, what am I doing?' to 'I think I might be okay.'"

No wonder Jewel was worried. Being the lead in a production was stressful. She didn't have a lot of free time to study her script, so she had to learn it on the road whenever she had a spare second. Since all the actors were so famous and, therefore, busy, there weren't even rehearsals. It was really weird for Jewel to practice just a few times with the director, just the two of them. The cast only rehearsed all together once, but the show went on as scheduled. Jewel's father came from Homer to see it. It was the first time he had ever visited New York City. (Not to be the last, with his rising star daughter.) *The Wizard of Oz* aired in November 1995 on TNT.

That night was a Jewel goldmine. Another show with much fanfare swept through national cable wires in the very same time slot (Jewel fans were disappointed because they couldn't watch both). It was VH1's *Duets,* a critically acclaimed program where Jewel performed with Melissa Etheridge.

* * *

On May 15, 1995, Jewel, still relatively unknown and with her single, "You Were Meant for Me," just above stagnating status on the hit charts, was invited to play on *Late Night with Conan O'Brian*. Right after the performance, her sluggish sales of five hundred CDs a week soared to nineteen hundred. That happened with one two-minute spot on national television while most of America silently slept. "When that red camera light went on, it was magic," said Shapiro. "We stood on the sidelines pinching ourselves, it was so extraordinary."

The small burst of success that came out of those few minutes led Atlantic to launch an aggressive TV tour with Jewel. It was tough, but the company's PR people doggedly sent out press releases to get Jewel more spots. Eventually, that effort added up to more than forty regional and national small-screen appearances—and those had to be worked into her already tight touring schedule. Atlantic never minded sending Jewel around the country and spending money on her career. She was a bargain to maintain. It wasn't like Jewel was going to ask to travel in a Mercedes tour bus. She was inexpensive, so they didn't mind sending her out once again.

It was the most profitable move that Atlantic could have made. Jewel performed on a slew of

TV shows. Within five months of taping *Conan,* she was asked to be on *The Tonight Show with Jay Leno, Good Morning America, VH1 Crossroads Live,* the morning program at KTVU-TV in San Francisco, *Much Music* in Canada, *CBS This Morning,* the *VH1 Top Video Countdown* from Vail, Colorado, which she cohosted, and *Late Night with David Letterman.* Those spots were just the beginning of Jewel's television career. Needless to say, her fifteen-thousand-dollar video for "Who Will Save Your Soul" was finally picked up by VH1.

Pieces of You flew off the racks. Jewel's mother called her right after Christmas that year to tell her she had sold nine thousand copies in one week. Jewel said, "If you're Alanis Morissette, it's totally dorky, right? But for me it was unbelievable." That moment, Jewel sat on her kitchen floor and cried. Her mom, on the other end of the phone, was crying, too. "It was very humbling," Jewel admitted.

Another break for Jewel came when a guy named Sean Penn called her up. He's the famous actor who was married to Madonna and has been in movies ranging from *Fast Times at Ridgemont High* to *Dead Man Walking.* He saw Jewel on *Conan* that night and was mesmerized. He was hell-bent on meeting Jewel, and when he did, they immediately started a whirlwind romance. Sean whisked Jewel off to the Venice Film Festival right around May 1995. While hanging out there, hand in hand, they started quite a buzz among the paparazzi and gossip columnists. Penn had fallen hard for yet another busty blond rocker girl—this time, it was our very own Jewel, who had just turned twenty-one. (Maybe his tastes had matured—after all, he went from the material girl to a neofolk singer.)

There was no denying the relationship, even though Jewel usually declined to talk about it with the press. It was actually very public during its short duration. For example, in September 1995, the New York *Daily News* reported a gossipy item about Penn that said he was caught in a lunchtime liplock with his longtime girlfriend and mother of his children, actress Robin Wright. The day the story ran, the *Daily News* got a call from Penn's less-than-pleased publicist, who insisted that the gossip item be corrected. Penn was *not* with Wright at lunch, Penn's publicist told the *Daily News*. He was *definitely* with Jewel, though, thank you. Here's what the *Daily News* had to say about the whole weird incident: "We're used to getting calls from publicists insisting their clients *are not* cheating on their wives or girlfriends (as the papers often report), especially with an actor like, say, Sean Penn. So imagine our shock when Penn's people called to correct [us, that he *was* kissing Jewel]."

Penn was sweet to Jewel when they were together. He even carried her guitars for her when she was on tour. Just by hanging out with him, Jewel got some of the exposure she so desperately needed at that time. Jewel wasn't worried about her talent being overshadowed by his star status, a silly gossip statement that newspapers liked to print. She said, "God, I don't get overly caught up in what people are going to think or not think. Whatever." Jewel got sick of reporters constantly asking her about the relationship, and she was never into answering questions about it.

Soon, Penn asked Jewel to record a song for his movie, *The Crossing Guard*. She *was* into that. He thought highly of Jewel and her talents, told all of his friends—and he has many—that Jewel was the next Dylan. He continued to praise Jewel's music even after they broke up. Penn went on to direct the first video version of Jewel's "You Were Meant for Me." The video aired only briefly on VH1. Atlantic pulled it when the grainy, low-budget "Who Will Save Your Soul" video surprisingly went into heavy telecast rotation on MTV and VH1. By the time they decided to rerelease the song "You Were Meant for Me," they had refilmed it. The new version starred another Jewel fan, Steve Poltz, and even though it may look that way on the video, the two were not seeing each other when it was made. As always, they are just good friends.

All in all, Penn and Jewel lasted less than a year. Penn dumped Jewel, heading back to Wright and marrying her. Jewel insists there are no hard feelings. She's never had nasty break-ups, opting to remain friends instead. Nor has she ever had a blowout fight with a boyfriend. According to those Jewel rules, Penn was treated no differently. Later, she recorded a song for another Penn film, *Dead Man Walking*.

Jewel may have been upset, but she's not one to sweat a guy. Besides, she would soon have another boyfriend to think about. She started seeing French-Canadian model Michel Francoeur in the spring of 1996. (They broke up in the spring of 1998, but they're still friends.) Jewel and he were spotted together lot. He's a gorgeous man, and a nice one, too, she says. When they first met, Jewel wasn't even famous, so they had to make some big adjustments. "It's strange for him. He's worried for me," she said at the time.

Jewel had too many good things going on to give men much brain time. Her success was growing—the overall musical climate was becoming Jewel-friendlier. And all the things that seemed so terribly wrong with her raw, honest album suddenly became so right. It's as if all the hard work finally became worth it; things—performances, tours, TV—just started to click.

In the beginning of 1996, people's attitudes about tunes were changing. Kurt Cobain had just committed suicide, and his death signaled the end of a grungy era. Music was about to get a makeover. A genre called modern adult contemporary was on the rise, with acts like Counting Crows and Blues Traveler. The format was female-friendly as well, lending itself to the Indigo Girls and Sarah MacLachlan, whose breakthrough album *Fumbling Towards Ecstasy* ended up going double platinum. One record exec puts the change nicely: "Honestly, we in the record business are not leaders. We are a bunch of sheep. When one kind of record does well, we all follow with more like it." In other words, it didn't hurt Jewel when Alanis Morissette took over the music scene, selling more than fifteen million copies of *Jagged Little Pill*.

Enter Jewel into the equation. It was her turn for a hit, even though she never expected one when she started the singing thing. As MacLachlan's manager, Terry McBride, said in July 1997, "Artists like Sarah, Fiona, and Jewel have always been at the bottom of the play lists, but about fourteen months ago, we started getting some attention. It helped all these artists get to the next step up."

Another realization at that time in the industry: women will buy music. They concluded that chick acts are profitable, as if it was some new revelation. Hello—female fans everywhere knew that a long time ago. Still, Jewel was shocked by the small surge of success she felt in mid-1995, but thrilled, too. The change in musical attitude was long overdue. "I think what people value now is starting to be sincerity. I also think you can't fight an enemy with despair, and the climate is really changing in music and what people want out of music."

If Jewel was delighted, then her breakthrough on the *Billboard* charts made Atlantic euphoric. Shapiro was very satisfied about the whole shebang, too, since promoting Jewel had been his baby. "Jewel breaking as an artist is one of the most satisfying moments of my professional career. . . . We brought through a difficult act and established a model with which to develop an artist on the road," he said. (Which means future artists need to bet on a long, Jewel-like tour before they even think about getting famous.)

Jewel sat in a Mexican restaurant in Columbia, South Carolina, having lunch with yet another reporter. She didn't mind, though, and laughingly described her complete story—tundra to present. Jewel was telling the woman about a scientist named Dr. Valerie Hunt. Jewel expressed her admiration for this amazing woman who had invented tools to measure brain waves. "Isn't that amazing?" Jewel said. She was excitedly sharing her story when the pair got interrupted. A man at the next table came up to Jewel and asked for her autograph. Jewel smiled. Then she admitted to the reporter that she'd never been approached in a restaurant before. She delightedly took care of the man's request.

11

A New Type of Fame

Jewel's tour, from early 1995 until early 1998, lasted a grueling, unprecedented three years. She traveled to every state and all over the world. In true Jewel style, she kept mementos from home with her no matter where she went. Jewel never wanted to forget where she had come from, who she was, and what inspired her in the first place. So she always carried a Tupperware container filled with her favorite things. The contents of the box consisted of an eagle feather, a photo of her van, a pinch of dirt, and some rocks from the homestead. Of course, Jewel also brings a pile of lovingly dog-eared Pablo Neruda, Proust, and Dostoyevsky books. The thoughts and feelings found in these personal mementos help the rising star to stay grounded. She often says she's not into the aggressive ways of the music industry. She said, "I don't adore 'the biz,' and I'm terrified of decadence, so I surround myself with what I know is real . . . and always remember to be joyous and thankful."

On the road, Jewel has had to search harder for silence, something that brings her peace and clearness of mind. "It was hard for me at first because, in Alaska, it was always so quiet." Silence practically doesn't exist on tour, not in the shared tour bus, certainly not at the nightly shows. Jewel said the lack was sometimes damaging to her spirit, "Touring can be draining . . . and it's never quiet. In silence we hear who we are going to become. We have to learn to listen for it. I've had to teach myself to hear that silence inside myself, no matter where I am."

Jewel was going places. With her naturally amazing voice and stage presence, she was outshining some headliners, such as Liz Phair. It wasn't much longer until Jewel opened gigs for John Hiatt, Neil Young, and even Bob Dylan. She'd hit the big time, and sometimes she was nervous about it. When she played with Neil Young in New York City's Madison Square Garden, she was extra antsy. Sensing Jewel's nervousness, Young gave her some prophetic advice: "Jewel, it's just another hash house on the road to success. Show it no respect."

Then there was Dylan. But she wasn't all that nervous about opening for the legend, except for a normal case of jitters. She said that after playing acoustic guitar between Everclear and Ramones sets, nothing was scary. Besides, by that time, she had already ruled the Garden. She was excited, though. Bob Dylan was an icon Jewel had looked up to for many, many years—what musician hasn't? Jewel had even been compared to him. She is a lot like the legend, a singer who totes a guitar and has been blessed with wicked songwriting skills. While opening his shows, she didn't even think she'd get to meet him. She thought wrong. Bob even went out to hear *her* sets. They talked at great length, and he offered her his guidance. The two got along great. "He's very honest; if he doesn't like you, he'll tell you. But he was so good to me." Bob Dylan encouraged Jewel, and at that time when she was teetering on the brink of success, she really needed it. "He told me to keep doing what I was doing and said I was very brave."

At one show, Bob asked Jewel to join him onstage. She was shocked. "I didn't even dare share his microphone until he waved me over. Afterward, he pushed me in front of the crowd and drawled: 'Heeeeeey . . . she sings bedder than Joan Buy-ezz,'" Jewel joked. Not only did Jewel receive sound advice from Dylan, she also perfected her hilarious Dylan impression. Oh, and she got to tweak his nose, too. (That's a little Jewel idiosyncrasy. She loves to do that to people as a sign of affection or admiration.) It was a great experience. What else would you do to such a distinguished legend, anyway? Jewel said, "Bob is so cool. I asked him if I could feel his nose, and he just leaned forward and presented it to me." That was one of Jewel's proudest moments on the tour.

Needless to say, acts like Duncan Sheik and Belly began opening for *her*. No longer did Jewel play coffeehouses, except for special, occasional visits that were mostly in San Diego. Her crowds had outgrown the nation's java joints. From now on, Jewel's gigs took place in large halls or on stages. After two years of "singing her brains out," Jewel's work finally got noticed. In fact, she became a certified star.

Next on her important agenda was playing at the presidential Inaugural Ball. Oh, nix that— Jewel actually played *two*. She met all of the politicians just a few months earlier, when she hosted an MTV show at the Democratic National Convention in late 1996 in Chicago. Then she was asked to provide entertainment for the last inaugural ball of the twentieth century. She spent time talking with Sheryl Crow, who was also performing, and the First Daughter herself. Sixteen-year-old Chelsea chatted with Jewel for quite a while. Jewel offered to send Chelsea her *Pieces of You* CD, but before she could finish, Chelsea told Jewel thanks, but she already owned it.

Awards shows invited Jewel to their gala events. She wasn't just a performer, either, she was a nominee. In early 1997, Jewel snagged the American Music Award for Favorite New Artist in the pop/rock category. Then, in March, she picked up the Blockbuster Award for Favorite New Female Artist. To top the year off, she was nominated for a pair of 1997 Grammy Awards in the categories of Best New Artist and Best Female Pop Vocal Performance for "Who Will Save Your Soul." She didn't win (she lost the first category to LeAnn Rimes), but just being nominated was a huge thrill. She didn't win the 1996 MTV Video Music Awards either the previous year, a bummer since she had been nominated for the awesome titles of Best Female Artist and Best New Artist. She was able to make up in the fall of 1997 for this loss when she performed at the MTV Video Music Awards and then won Best Female Performance in a Video for "You Were Meant for Me."

Jewel was amazed. When the album came out

in early 1995, she never dreamed that she'd be sitting pretty at the Grammys two years later.

Well, maybe she sat a little too pretty. There was a mistake that Jewel made when she attended the prestigious show that night. A *Rolling Stone* writer described the situation best: "Despite the appearance of such ceremony newcomers as Beck, Hillary Clinton, and *Jewel's nipples,* it was a very traditional Grammy night." Jewel made quite an impression, to say the least. She showed up in a fourteen-thousand-dollar loaner from chic designer Gianfranco Ferre. Only she hadn't exactly put on an expensive bra. Jewel basically went au naturel to the show. And her fans could see everything. She wasn't pulling a Cher or anything; she really didn't know she was giving millions of viewers a peep show. In response to all the media hype, Jewel proved that she can take a joke. She explained, "The whole thing was hilarious. The dress. I tried it on in a hotel room that wasn't backlit. You're in a dress, you feel like an angel. I didn't have an entire spotlight up my [butt]." To this day, she still hasn't looked at the video tape. Jewel just isn't into all that fashion stuff, anyway. Just before the Grammys, when the paparazzi and reporters were buzzing out front, someone asked Jewel which designer she was wearing. Dior? Prada? Jewel's answer, "Farrah . . . I can't remember." (That same reporter asked Jewel what she'd been listening to on her CD player lately. Jewel told her she didn't have one. "I have a book," she explained. "I'm reading Octavio Paz and Anne Dillard.")

That wasn't the first time Jewel caused a stir at an awards program. She caused another reaction a year earlier. In April 1996, Jewel was asked to sing at the Michael Awards in New York City—they're practically the Oscars of fashion. She belted out her song "Pieces of You" to the crowd. The song contains lyrics like "You say he's a faggot, does it make you want to hurt him?" and "You say he's a Jew, does it mean that he's tight?" The largely gay and Jewish audience in attendance didn't exactly get or appreciate the song's antihate message. Instead, they were angry. Later, Jewel defended herself: "It's a shame if anyone thinks I'm a racist or homophobe. That song's about the absence of fear and ignorance. Say the words, and they lose the strength they've been given."

One of the night's coordinators wasn't too happy about it. She was going to bring in Joan Osborne but was afraid Osborne's God song would offend Catholics. She said, "You just can't win. I love Jewel's song, but it might not have been the most appropriate song to sing at this event." Of course, Jewel meant no harm. She's merely a sincere social crusader who later admitted, "Well, I kinda couldn't resist getting a reaction."

Next stop, *Time* magazine. All the awards, exposure, and awesome concerts landed Jewel some major magazine exposure. Most notably, she graced the cover of one of the nation's most respected news magazines, *Time,* in the July 21, 1997, issue. The mag rarely runs pop culture on its covers, but Jewel was that big. During the summer of 1997, Jewel moved up a notch from star to superstar, evident from her unique beauty staring at America from every grocery store shelf. That summer, she was the cover girl for other cool mags, too, like *Rolling Stone, Details,* and *US;* and she was featured on the inside pages of just about every other magazine on the planet.

She became a media diva. Though exhausted from constant touring—on air and on the road—she'd spend her precious days off, or times between shows, with reporters. She mastered the whole interview process. She created moods, dodged questions she didn't care for with finesse (like those about her and Sean Penn), and endeared reporters and readers to her quirky qualities. When *Rolling Stone*'s writer came to interview Jewel, the singer created an intimate setting. After a show in Denver, the reporter showed up at Jewel's hotel room and knocked at her door. Jewel peeped out and said, "Are you wearing pajamas? Good. Come on in." Jewel sat on her bed with her guitar in hand as she got ready to answer the usual questions. She turned out the lights, opting for a candle as the reporter started asking, "Where did you grow up? What was it like without electricity?" and so on. Jewel joked and remained light-hearted before calling it a night at three A.M. The two met again the next day to continue their conversation.

Often, Jewel starts interviews by interviewing the interviewer. It's not unusual for her to greet reporters with her own set of questions, like "What's your middle name?" "What's your sign?" "What's your favorite food and why?" She's naturally curious and loves to chat. Jewel's also eager to learn about people, even the thousands of reporters who've pursued her. As much as she likes the attention, there's another side of being famous: endlessly telling your life's story isn't the easiest way to get through the week, she admitted. "You talk your guts out. Your nerve endings are shot, and you're totally useless as a human being." Jewel has learned to deal—she's now had time to adjust. "This is my life now. The amount I'm getting out of it personally and what I'm learning has made me grow by leaps and bounds."

That is her goal, to learn to handle fame and

fortune with dignity and a sense of humor. She often says that if she doesn't keep her spirit intact, then none of the success is worth it. One of the ways she accomplishes that goal is by ignoring the media frenzy that constantly surrounds her. Half the time, she won't even read the articles or watch the programs that are about her. "Sometimes it just affects me," she said. So far, Jewel's been able to keep herself happy, something many new stars just can't do. Her long stretches of good health—minus the kidney problems—are proof that Jewel can take care of herself, inside and out.

12

Loving Lilith

In the Hebrew legend, Lilith was Adam's first wife. She wasn't one bit like Eve, who was created from Adam's rib. Lilith was Adam's equal; God created them separately. When he joined the two together, they incessantly quarreled. Adam told Lilith, "It is your duty to obey me." Lilith replied, "We are both equal . . . and I will not be submissive to you."

With that story in mind, Sarah MacLachlan created the Lilith Fair. She wanted to give summer concertgoers a choice besides the hard-hitting, male-dominated Lollapalooza-type shows. She had a vision—all of the talented women she admired could tour together and put on incredible shows across the country. They could share their music with each other and with the world. When she got those women together—Fiona

115

Apple, Meredith Brooks, Erykah Badu, Sheryl Crow, Paula Cole, Shawn Colvin, and many others—their joint efforts became surprise sell-outs. When Sarah had first publicized her idea for the tour, the media pretty much laughed it off as a bunch of chicks who'd never be able to fill a stadium. But Sarah didn't care. The show wasn't about ticket sales or exposure. It was about camaraderie and intimacy. And with those good intentions, the Lilith Fair ended up with sky-rocket ticket sales that made it the highest-grossing tour of the summer.

Jewel was there, too. She played the majority of the nationwide dates, sandwiching Lilith between her own Tiny Lights Tour. She often stole Lilith. At the end of each night, the performers came onstage to sing together for the audience. It wasn't unusual for Jewel to take the lead. At the end of one show, she belted out Joni Mitchell's "Big Yellow Taxi" with the ladies of Lilith as backup. Jewel's career had been going very well, with swelling sales of *Pieces of You,* but Lilith definitely gave the album yet another push that it needed. Of course, that's not the reason Jewel participated in Lilith; she was wholeheartedly behind Sarah MacLachlan's ideals. But as a result of the success of the concert, Jewel appeared on the cover of *Time,* as mentioned earlier, and even more fans took notice of her music—and bought it.

At the same time, though, Jewel just loved the camaraderie of the tour and the feelings that they, as artists, were able to evoke in their crowds. Audiences—women, couples, teen girls, and rebel bands of a few men—poured into summer amphitheaters. Everyone was caught up in Lilith's power. Jewel attributes the show's success to the awesome emotions the music could evoke. "People are hungry for emotiveness. They want bare honesty, emotional blood-and-bone honesty," she said. Jewel was touched as well. After touring like crazy for two years, Lilith brought welcome changes. Like, say, a few female friends that Jewel had a lot in common with. "Usually you're so lonely on the road, like a little astronaut. We had a real sense of community. None of us wanted to leave," she said.

Right after Lilith, Jewel hopped a plane to go to Europe. Touring foreign countries where she was a total unknown would be nothing like Lilith. Jewel felt very alone once she arrived. She was only halfheartedly joking when she told her friends that she was about to embark on her "suicide mission." Friends were concerned. One came up to her after a summer show and asked her about it. She answered that she'd had only four weeks off in the last two and a half years. Then the acquaintance replied, "Don't you need a vacation?" Her answer: "I'm only twenty-three. I have the rest of my life to vacation." She spent the last months of 1997 in Europe—it was her third tour there. And when she returned to the States, it was finally time for a break. After almost three years, the long, hard tour for her first album, *Pieces of You,* came to an end.

13

The Future

Jewel is way famous now, but she still doesn't believe it. Her awe-inspiring success and stardom just don't seem real sometimes. Those days of peanut butter and carrots may not ever escape Jewel's memory—nor will that sense of panic that she once felt when she wasn't happy with her life. Those experiences are far more deeply ingrained in Jewel's brain than the superstardom will ever be. And she wants to keep herself grounded in that way, by remembering her life and its hardships. Jewel will never have to worry about money again; she's loaded. That's a little hard to believe, too. In August 1997, she told *US* magazine, "Even when I was living in my car, I hoped I would get to do what I loved. I never thought it would be on this level. I don't mean so much the level of success but the actualization of knowing that for the rest of my life, I'm going to be OK. That's so amazing to get used to."

Jewel's a very real person, superstar or not. She doesn't have celebrity fixations like having to be accompanied at all times by an entourage of stylists and makeup artists. That's not Jewel. She doesn't have a drug or alcohol problem— she doesn't touch either one and said, "It has never interested me, anyway." She doesn't have sexy male groupies and doesn't throw wild rock parties in hotels after her shows. She trades them both in for quiet nights. Jewel said she likes to go back to her hotel and put on her pajamas. Sometimes the stress of it all gets to her, though. Jewel cried after one of her biggest shows ever in Los Angeles in the summer of '97. That night, she endured hours of schmoozy meet-and-greet with tons of radio programmers and video promotions people. The pressure was just too much. She broke down in tears, and when the event ended, she left with her boyfriend Michel to try to get some sleep.

Jewel insists that she remains raw and unpolished. When she was named one of *People* magazine's most amazing people of 1997, she said, "I'm not hip, I'm not produced, I'm not slick. I don't have a big image thing." Even when Jewel performed at the 1998 SuperBowl in San Diego in front of her biggest ever crowd—one billion people worldwide—she slipped into the stadium and then out as quietly as possible. There was some question about whether she sang the anthem live or not. On television, it looked as though the singing started before Jewel opened her mouth. Jewel's mom admitted that the national anthem wasn't sung live at all; it was prerecorded against Jewel's wishes, and she had asked to sing it live. The NFL decided not to let her because of sound technicalities. In an even greater technical difficulty, Jewel started lip-synching too late (which wasn't entirely her fault; the TV people played the anthem twenty seconds before they were supposed to). Regardless, she said, "I like what my voice did with the high notes, and I think it's also sexy—the low notes. I wanted it to be elegant."

So what, she missed a cue? She hates it when the media, and people in general, treat her like a superhero. Jewel doesn't appreciate attention that puts her on a beyond-human pedestal. "People look in magazines and feel like I'm a phenomenon, as if what I've accomplished is beyond their ability. I tell them to knock it off. If you respect what I've done, then do something yourself."

* * *

In November of 1998, Jewel's new CD (still untitled at press time) will "drop," as they say in the music industry. It will be a Christmas-y album. "I'm not going to sing 'Jingle Bells,'" Jewel explained. "It will be all original songs, kind of inspirational. . . . It will be uplifting." No one can wait to hear it. It was first scheduled to hit stores in January 1996. Obviously, it didn't. Whenever another song off *Pieces of You* did well, Atlantic postponed her new album. Jewel even went into the studio several times to record new music, but each time, Atlantic scrapped the idea in favor of promoting songs like "Foolish Games." Wise move. That song, which started out as a real chart sleeper, ended up with a record-breaking sixty-five-plus consecutive weeks on the *Billboard* Hot 100 charts. Jewel broke the Beatles' previous records for their songs "Can't Buy Me Love," and "Penny Lane," both of which had stayed on the charts for ten-week consecutive runs. Beating any record set by the Beatles was a prestigious accomplishment for Jewel. (Actually, "You Were Meant for Me" broke the record first, spending fifty-nine weeks on the Hot 100 chart.) As for her album, at press time it had sold more than eight million copies and had gone platinum eight times.

What will be on her next album? She has said it will be more diverse. "It will have some blues and jazz and more rock stuff, along with the acoustic stuff. It'll be kind of flirtatious, but not folk rock." No matter what it is, millions of fans can't wait to hear for themselves.

In the summer of 1997, a reporter asked Jewel where she saw herself in five years. Her answer was, "I hope to be in other art fields by then. Movies. I definitely want to have a poetry book by then." She was predicting the future, so a new CD is only the beginning of what to expect from Jewel in upcoming months. She's already written a book of poetry called *A Night without Armor* that hit the best-seller list last spring along with a CD of Jewel reading her prose. About her poetry, she says, "I'm always looking at who I am, who I've been, and who I'm going to be. And I think poetry was always my first instinct. I can't live without writing poetry." With her book, she hopes to inspire young people to get into poetry—and start writing their own. Also, look for a scapbook/memoir book in the fall of 1998, scheduled to come out with her new Christmas album. (She was offered a whopping two million dollars to write those books.)

For the second time since *Wizard of Oz,* Jewel's going to shine as a star. This time as the female lead in a thirty-five-million-dollar Hollywood production. Last spring, she started filming a movie tentatively titled *Ride with the Devil,* an epic tale of the Civil War based on the novel *Woe to Live On.* She'll be the lucky love interest of both Tobey Maguire and Skeet Ulrich. The two cute dudes play Missouri farm boys who become Confederate guerrillas in the horrible warfare. During filming in Kansas City, Jewel was asked if she minded working with mostly men. She laughed and answered, "That's the fun part!"

The movie, directed by Ang Lee *(The Ice Storm, Sense and Sensibility,* and *Eat Drink Man Woman),* almost starred Leonardo Di-Caprio and Matt Damon. They pulled out, citing "other commitments," and the production company, Fox Searchlight, dropped out. For a while, the movie was in trouble, then Universal Studios took on the film, backing it with loads of cash. The show went on. And it's scheduled to be in theaters in the fall of 1999.

Initial problems dealt with, Lee says he is thrilled to work with Jewel in her movie debut. He describes her perfectly: "Jewel is the perfect mixture of down-to-earth and ethereal." And Jewel couldn't be happier about the part. She puts it best: "I'm really looking forward to having my [butt] kicked by a new challenge. For me, singing and songwriting utilize only one part of a very creative body." More stuff from Jewel will be very cool.

It looks like Jewel's awesome journey has just begun.

Pieces of Jewel: Bonus FAQs

Top 10 Jewel Web Sites

If you need a Jewel fix, the Web can be a bit overwhelming. There are more than one hundred Jewel sites. Here's our guide to the best of the best.

1. Pieces of Jewel

Everything Jewel you could ever want or ask for; interesting pictures, facts, and tour dates—a must for every Jewel fan.
http://jewel.zoonation.com

2. Official Jewel Web Site

Accept no imitations! Includes tour dates, little-known facts, video info, pictures, the Jewel store (lots of cool Jewel stuff).
http://www.jeweljk.com

3. Atlantic Records

Atlantic's official site. Totally out of date but worth checking out.
http://www.atlantic-records.com

4. The Jewel Shrine

Tons of cool pictures, a chat room, and even lyrics to unreleased songs.
http://www.wantree.com.au/~awatson/ jewel.htm

5. Gerrit's Jewel Links

This Web-ster claims to have a link to "every Jewel site in existence"; he's not lying.
http://www.endor.org/jewel/links

6. EDA Jewel Mailing List and Member Guide

Very cool mailing list info, tons of pictures, cool links. It's all here—all the names and stuff you should know, cool Jewel vocab and facts.
http://www.spectra.net/~ducksoup

7. Jewel

Awesome, high-quality photos, like Jewel at the Grammys and in the back of her VW van. Available in black and white or color.
http://users.cougar.net/~dja5/jewel

8. Jewel Guitar Tabs Page

Play Jewel's songs on *your* guitar.
http://www.mindspring.com/~hiakia/jewel_tabs

9. Albert Wang's Jewel Page

Quotations, interviews, and Quicktime mov-

ie links grace this Jewel page, a place for Jewel philosophers.
http://hugse1.harvard.edu/~wangal/jewel.html

10. Jewel Audio Only Page

Download your favorite Jewel song or video on this fab Web site (not for the computer-illiterate).
http://members.aol.com/jewelpage/index.htm

Stuff you *must* know about Jewel:

Birthdate: May 23, 1974
Sign: Taurus
Eyes: Hazel
Height: 5'4"

• Jewel has the coolest fan club on the planet. They're called the EDAs, or Every Day Angels (their name comes from a line in Jewel's *Pieces of You* song "I'm Sensitive"). They started an online mailing list when Jewel began her awesome career in San Diego. As Jewel's name spread across the world, so did the Web-based EDA membership. Jewel's so into them—her most faithful, oldest fans—that she even put on a free EDA-only concert for them near Woodstock, New York, in the summer of 1996. EDAs gathered from across the country to attend and bond (Jewel even sat down to eat a spaghetti dinner with a bunch of them). Today, the EDAs are stronger than ever. Jewel keeps in touch with them, occasionally sending them loving e-mails. To become an EDA, join their online e-mail list. (P.S. It's hectic, like fifty-plus e-mails a day.) Go to **http://www.spectra.net/~ducksoup** for instructions.

* There is a star in the northern skies named for Jewel Kilcher. The EDAs gave it to her for her twenty-third birthday.

* Jewel Kilcher has no middle name, but Jewel is the name she was born with.

* Jewel and Flea from the Red Hot Chili Peppers are great friends. They met way before Jewel was famous, though, when Jewel was still living out of her van. He just went for a walk and saw this gorgeous girl and went to chat. "She said to me, 'Let me play you a few songs on my guitar,' " Flea said. "I thought, 'Oh no.' But she did it, and it was so incredibly beautiful. It turns out later that she became a big star."

**Think you know everything about
today's hottest heartthrob,
Leonardo DiCaprio?
It's time to take the *ultimate* test of
Leo trivia and see if you're truly his
number-one fan!**

POP
Quiz:
Leonardo DiCaprio

Nancy Krulik

**With a special fold-out poster
of Leo!**

Coming in mid-October 1998

**From Archway Paperback
Published by Pocket Books**

2019